D1563582

The Economics of
Mutual Fund Markets:
Competition Versus Regulation

ROCHESTER STUDIES IN ECONOMICS
AND POLICY ISSUES

Series Editors:

Karl Brunner and Paul W. MacAvoy
University of Rochester
Rochester, New York, USA

Previously published books in the series:

1. Brunner, K.: *Economics and Social Institutions*
2. Brunner, K.: *The Great Depression Revisited*
3. McCormick, R., and Tollison, R.: *Politicians, Legislation, and the Economy*
4. Rasche, R.: *Controlling the Growth of Monetary Aggregates*
5. MacAvoy, P.: *Explaining Metals Prices*
6. MacAvoy, P., Stanbury, W., Yarrow, G., and Zeckhauser, R.: *Privatization and State-Owned Enterprises*

Published in cooperation with

The Bradley Policy Research Center
William E. Simon Graduate School
of Business Administration
University of Rochester
Rochester, New York

The Economics of
Mutual Fund Markets:
Competition Versus Regulation

William J. Baumol
New York University
Princeton University

Stephen M. Goldfeld
Princeton University

Lilli A. Gordon
Analysis Group, Inc.

Michael F. Koehn
Analysis Group, Inc.
University of California, Irvine

Kluwer Academic Publishers
Boston   Dordrecht   London

Distributors

for North America: Kluwer Academic Publishers,
101 Philip Drive, Assinippi Park, Norwell, Massachusetts 02061 USA

for all other countries: Kluwer Academic Publishers Group
Distribution Centre, Post Office Box 322, 3300 AH Dordrecht,
THE NETHERLANDS

Library of Congress Cataloging-in-Publication Data

The Economics of mutual fund markets : competition versus regulation /
   William J. Baumol ... [et al.].
      p.   cm. — (Rochester studies in economics and policy issues ;
  v. 7)
   Includes bibliographical references.
   ISBN 0-7923-9043-1
   1. Mutual funds. I. Baumol, William J. II. Series.
  HG4530.E26   1989
  332.63′27—dc20   89-19857
                                               CIP

The opinions contained in this book are based on the authors' independent interpretation of publicly available information. These opinions
should not be regarded as factual or definitive in nature.

The information contained in this report is taken from publicly available
sources. The authors and Publisher make no claims, express or implied,
as to the accuracy of the information and assume no liability for any
consequences resulting from its use.

TP

TABLE OF CONTENTS

ONE: HISTORY OF THE DEVELOPMENT OF THE MUTUAL FUND INDUSTRY

TWO: REGULATION OF THE MUTUAL FUND INDUSTRY

THREE: LITIGATION UNDER THE 1940 ACT AND
THE 1970 AMENDMENTS

FOUR: ANALYSIS OF THE ADVISER-SHAREHOLDER
RELATIONSHIP IN THE MUTUAL FUND INDUSTRY

FIVE: A STUDY OF CURRENT MARKET
CONDITIONS IN THE MUTUAL FUND INDUSTRY

SIX: THE DEMAND FOR MONEY MARKET MUTUAL FUNDS

SEVEN: A COST STUDY OF MUTUAL FUND COMPLEXES

EIGHT: TOWARD RATIONAL POLICY ON
REGULATION OF MUTUAL FUNDS

LIST OF FIGURES

LIST OF TABLES

The Economics of
Mutual Fund Markets:
Competition Versus Regulation

PREFACE

The original impetus for this research was provided several years ago by a request to assist Counsel for Fidelity Management and Research Corporation in analyzing the mutual fund industry, with particular emphasis on money market mutual funds. We were asked to focus our efforts on the mechanism by which the advisory fees of mutual funds are determined. This request arose out of litigation that challenged the level of advisory fees charged to the shareholders of the Fidelity Cash Reserve Fund. Subsequently, we were asked to provide similar assistance to Counsel for T. Rowe Price Associates regarding the fees charged to shareholders of their Prime Reserve Fund.

Under the Investment Company Act of 1940, advisers of mutual funds have a fiduciary duty with respect to the level of fees they may charge a fund's shareholders. Since the passage of the Investment Company Act, there have been numerous lawsuits brought by shareholders alleging that advisory fees were excessive. In these lawsuits, the courts have failed to provide a set of standards for determining when such fees are excessive. Instead, they have relied on arbitrary and frequently ill-defined criteria for judging the reasonableness of fees. This failure to apply economic-based tests for evaluating the fee structure of mutual funds provided the motivation for the present book, which undertakes a comprehensive analysis of the economics of the mutual fund industry.

Our research has benefited greatly from the stimulating ideas provided by James Ditmar and Richard Lavin, Counsel for Fidelity, and by Henry Hopkins, Daniel Pollack, and Martin Kaminsky, Counsel for T. Rowe Price. Our efforts on behalf of Fidelity and T. Rowe Price resulted in much of the background analyses and data collection on money market mutual funds. The analysis was subsequently expanded to include the entire mutual fund industry.

While space does not permit individual recognition of all those who were instrumental in the completion of this effort, we wish to express our appreciation for their assistance. There are, however, several individuals who should be singled out for their considerable contributions. We would like to thank Paul MacAvoy for his extremely valuable comments. We are indebted to Charles Wittenberg for his extensive research on the legislative history of the 1940 Investment Company Act and on court cases relating to mutual fund fees. Special thanks are also due to Eric Wruck for his efforts on the statistical analysis and to Linda Lynch, Fred Ingham, and Laura Cook, who oversaw production of various drafts of the book.

INTRODUCTION

Since the passage of the Investment Company Act of 1940 (*ICA* or *1940 Act*), and indeed since well before that time, the economic behavior of investment companies has been the subject of often acrimonious debate. The debate has focused on whether the structure of investment companies leads to exploitation of mutual fund shareholders and excessive profits for the mutual fund industry. Industry critics have for many decades claimed that the complexity of financial markets, coupled with the structure of mutual funds themselves, leads inevitably to abusive behavior. The core of their arguments has been the behavior of fund advisers, who are alleged to have sufficient power to make shareholders their captives, and thereby to earn excessive fees for their management services. The industry has thus been viewed as lacking the essential competitive safeguards that prevent abuse of consumers.

The debate has resulted in a regulatory and legal framework that has been influential in determining the structure, conduct, and performance of the industry in the period since the Second World War. Laws and regulations have focused primarily on limiting the potential for mutual fund advisers to abuse shareholders, and thereby to earn excessive profits. The legal and regulatory structure has placed constraints on how funds and their advisers set their fees. In addition, the regulatory structure has imposed a series of costly strictures on mutual fund corporate structure. In particular, the Investment Company Act mandates that mutual funds be structured as corporations, with boards that include outside directors purportedly serving as a check on managerial discretion.

As this regulatory structure has evolved, and as a series of legal precedents has further limited the behavior of mutual fund advisers, remarkably little evidence has been offered to justify the restrictions imposed on the mutual fund industry. This book attempts to fill that void. We examine, both conceptually and empirically, the economic merit of the arguments advanced in support of the current regulatory and legal structure. We offer evidence on the behavior of the industry, the behavior of mutual fund consumers, and the consequent ability of advisers to charge excessive fees.

This book presents a detailed account of the regulatory, legal, and economic history of the mutual fund industry. It then examines the industry as it exists today and discusses how the current structure and economic conditions influence inter-actions between mutual fund advisers and shareholders as well as the ability of fund advisers to abuse shareholders. We assess the merits of the existing regulatory structure in view of the economic behavior of the industry and conclude with a discussion of proposed policy changes, which in our view would increase the efficiency of the mutual fund industry. The book is organized as follows.

Chapter One describes the development of the mutual fund industry. It considers the evolution of the industry in three distinct stages. The first stage, which corresponds to the pre-1940 period, marked the infancy of the mutual fund industry, and was characterized mainly by a small number of closed-end investment companies. In the second stage, from 1940-1970, the industry underwent rapid growth with respect to the level of assets invested as well as the number of share-holder accounts and the number of mutual funds. In the third stage, from 1970 to the present, the industry continued to grow, but exhibited a degree of innovation that had not been witnessed in the preceding two stages.

Chapter Two analyzes the regulation of the mutual fund industry, beginning with the period leading to the adoption of the Investment Company Act of 1940 and ending with recent regulatory initiatives within the industry. This chapter thoroughly reviews the rationale given for regulation of the mutual fund industry and the specific regulatory mechanisms that were adopted to safeguard shareholders against potentially abusive behavior. Chapter Two thus provides the necessary framework for assessing the key question — is regulation of the mutual fund industry called for in the current market environment?

Just as important as the regulatory structure that guides the industry are the legal standards that determine how the regulations ultimately are enforced. Chapter Three examines in detail the litigation brought under the ICA and the subsequent 1970 Amendments. It concludes with a discussion of the actual and implicit economic theories that have been applied in the course of mutual fund litigation.

Chapters Four through Seven focus on the industrial economics of the mutual fund industry. The analyses contained in these chapters directly challenge traditional views regarding the potential for mutual fund advisers to abuse shareholders by charging excessive management fees. Chapter Four presents an analysis of the adviser-shareholder relationship in the mutual fund industry. It describes in detail the characteristics of transactions between shareholders in a fund and the fund's adviser. The chapter also discusses the role of competition as a restraining force in the determination of advisory fees and identifies the questions that must be addressed in assessing the fee-setting behavior of mutual fund advisers.

Chapter Five is a study of current market conditions in the mutual fund industry. It seeks to determine whether the forces of competition are sufficiently strong to deter mutual fund advisers from behaving in a manner contrary to the best interests of shareholders. After applying the standard set of economic tests, we find that the industry is highly competitive and that the structure of transactions between advisers and shareholders combined with a high degree of shareholder mobility precludes mutual fund advisers from charging excessive fees.

Chapter Six provides additional evidence on the competitive strength of the mutual fund industry. In this chapter, we test empirically the often-expressed view that mutual fund advisers are in the enviable position of being able to set fees that are excessively high with little or no risk of driving away their customers. The chapter presents a statistical analysis of consumer demand for money market mutual funds and measures the degree of money market mutual fund shareholder sensitivity both to changes in relative net yield and to the total fees of a fund. We find that a proportionate increase in the total fees of a fund will lead to a more than proportionate loss in that fund's market share.

Chapter Seven investigates in detail the cost structure of the mutual fund industry in an attempt to assess directly the validity of views about the cost structure that have influenced regulatory policies. This chapter closely examines the notion of economies of scale as it applies to mutual fund complexes. Our empirical analysis suggests evidence of overall economies of scale as well as economies of scope with respect to the supply of money market and non-money market mutual funds. We discuss the implications of these findings and how they bear on the regulatory and legal structure of the mutual fund industry.

Chapter Eight summarizes our findings on the economic behavior of the industry. It then discusses the implications of these findings for law and regulation. We assess the merits of the current structure and propose changes that would, in our view, increase the efficiency of the mutual fund market.

Overall, our findings suggest that much of the existing regulatory framework governing mutual fund behavior is misdirected. The industry appears to be strongly competitive, with few barriers to entry by new mutual fund companies and advisers, and very low costs to consumers of switching among funds. These factors imply that there is no need for rigid structures governing either mutual fund activity or the relationship between funds and their advisers. Accordingly, in Chapter Eight, we recommend elimination of these structures — both governmental and corporate — and stress the need for continued and improved disclosure. We suggest that, given the competitive nature of the industry, consumers are better protected by the provision of full and clear information than by any particular structure for mutual fund companies or the fee-setting process.

ONE

HISTORY OF THE DEVELOPMENT OF THE MUTUAL FUND INDUSTRY

INTRODUCTION

Evaluating the regulatory measures that affect the mutual fund industry requires a complete examination of the historical and actual structure of the mutual fund industry, the mode of operation of the funds, and the behavior of mutual fund shareholders. The stated purpose of current regulatory measures, primarily those embodied in the 1940 Investment Company Act and the subsequent 1970 Amendments, is to protect shareholders of mutual funds and of other types of investment companies from abuse by a company's management. Before the passage of the ICA, mutual fund investors had little regulatory protection from alleged unscrupulous management, and alleged abuse of shareholders was persistently reported. Since the passage of the ICA and the 1970 Amendments, however, there have been significant changes in the organizational structure of investment companies, as well as in the economic structure of the mutual fund industry. It is particularly important, then, to examine whether these changes have altered the prospects for abuse and thereby affected the appropriate regulatory policy. The purpose of this chapter is to describe the overall development and the pertinent changes in the industry.

The mutual fund industry evolved in three stages: pre-1940, 1940-1970, and 1970 to the present. These stages coincide with the passage of the ICA and the subsequent 1970 Amendments. Table 1.1 compares how such relevant characteristics as the predominant structure, size, growth rate, and types of investment objectives of an investment company differed across the three stages.

The first stage, the period before 1940, was the infancy of the mutual fund industry. The early management companies, created at the turn of the twentieth century, were small, dissimilar, and frequently formed for purposes other than the provision of a diversified investment portfolio to the public. The first organizational form of investment company to achieve wide public acceptance was the closed-end fund. These funds are similar to the mutual funds of today, but unlike mutual funds, they do not offer new shares continuously nor are they obligated to redeem shares. Rather, investors trade shares in closed-end funds on the stock exchanges or in the over-the-counter market.

Before 1940, closed-end funds accounted for the majority of the assets invested through investment companies. In 1929, they accounted for 95 percent of total assets. By 1940, open-end or mutual funds had begun to replace closed-end funds as the preferred investment company vehicle. In 1940, shareholders had invested $450 million in assets with 68 separate mutual funds, and the share accounted for by closed-end funds had fallen to 57.5 percent.

In the second stage, between 1940 and 1970, mutual funds evolved into an established industry. During this stage, there was rapid and steady growth in mutual fund assets, the number of funds, and the number of shareholder accounts. Assets increased more than 100 fold, from $450 million to $47.6 billion. This increase is approximately the same as that which would have occurred had the entire $450 million been invested in the Standard and Poor market basket. For comparison, we note that from 1940 to 1970 the consumer price index rose by a factor of three, while the amount of mortgage debt outstanding rose by a factor of 13. During the same time, the

Table 1.1

Characteristics of the Investment Company Industry

Characteristic	Pre-1940	1940-1970	1970-1987
Range of closed-end funds:			
Total assets ($ billions)	0 - 0.61	0.61 - 4.0	4.0 - 20.5
Range of open-end funds:			
Number of funds	0 - 68	68 - 361	361 - 2,324
Number of accounts (millions)	0 - 0.30	0.30 - 10.7	10.7 - 54.6
Total assets ($ billions)	0 - 0.45	0.45 - 47.6	47.6 - 769.9
Average annual growth rates of open-end funds:			
Number of funds	NA	5.7%	11.6%
Number of accounts	NA	12.7%	10.1%
Total assets	NA	16.8%	17.8%
Predominant fund structure	Closed-end	Open-end	Open-end
Investment objectives	Equity-oriented	- Aggressive growth - Growth - Growth and income - Balanced - Income	- 5 objective types in 1970 - 22 objective types in 1987

Sources: Investment Company Institute, Mutual Fund Fact Book, 1984-1988 editions; "The Mutual Fund Industry: A Legal Survey," Notre Dame Lawyer, vol. 44 (1968-1969), 782; Wiesenberger Financial Services, Investment Companies (1976).

number of funds available to investors increased by a factor of five, from 68 to 361. The number of shareholder accounts grew to 10.7 million. During this stage, the mutual fund, also known as an open-end fund, became the most prevalent form of investment company. The number of investment objectives was small, with most funds being equity-oriented.

A distinguishing characteristic of the third stage, the post-1970 period, has been the proliferation of investment objectives. Up until this stage, mutual funds were almost exclusively equity funds organized to give small investors access to diversified portfolios and professional money management. As the industry matured, fund managers offered funds with a greater diversity of objectives. While there were five types of funds offered in 1970, there were 22 different types in 1987.[1] Much of this increase was the result of true innovation in objective types, although refinement of the classification system has also played a role in increasing the number of recognized mutual fund investment objectives.

The emergence of the first money market mutual fund in the early 1970s was an important innovation in the industry. The money market fund is fundamentally different from the typical equity fund. In many respects, a money market fund more closely resembles a NOW account offered by banks, which is an account that can be used as both a savings vehicle and as a means to make transactions. Following the innovative lead of money market funds, managers introduced a wide variety of new funds in the late 1970s and early 1980s in an effort to hold on to current investors and to attract new ones as equity and bond market conditions changed. Another striking feature of this third stage has been the emergence of families of mutual funds, or complexes, that provide investors with valuable exchange privileges utilizing the services of many different funds. The deregulation of the banking industry during this period has also had a significant influence on the

---

[1] These categories are based on the classifications of the Investment Company Institute.

evolution of mutual funds, a development that is described more fully below.

To comprehend the magnitude of the changes in the mutual fund industry, it is helpful to quantify industry growth as measured by the increase in fund assets. The growth has been achieved primarily through new investment in mutual funds, but also through capital appreciation of funds' existing assets. Only $140 million was invested in mutual funds in 1929 (see Figure 1.1). By the end of 1987, that amount had grown to almost $770 billion. This growth represents an average annual increase of 16 percent.

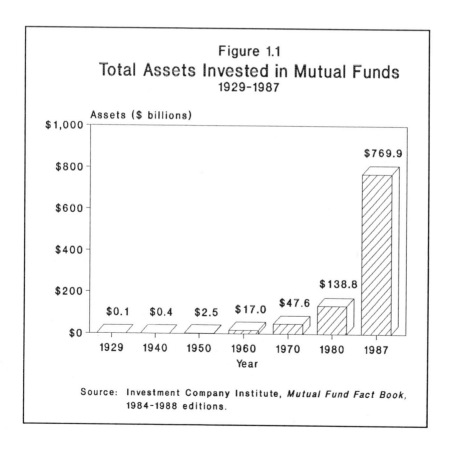

Figure 1.1
Total Assets Invested in Mutual Funds
1929-1987

Source: Investment Company Institute, *Mutual Fund Fact Book*, 1984-1988 editions.

Along with growth in assets, the number of mutual funds and individual shareholder accounts have increased steadily. As shown in Figure 1.2, the number of funds grew from 19 in 1929 to 2,324 by the end of 1987. Similarly, Figure 1.3 reports that the number of accounts has increased from 50,000 in 1929 to 54.6 million by the end of 1987.

Continuing innovation in the industry, which has enabled it to sustain significant growth over an extended length of time, has also fundamentally altered the opportunities available to small investors. This chapter provides a detailed examination of the sources of innovation and the ways in which investment companies have evolved during the three stages of the industry's development.

INVESTMENT COMPANIES

Organizational Structure

An understanding of the organizational structure of an investment company is needed to evaluate claims that this structure has prevented arm's-length bargaining between a fund and its adviser, leading to expropriation of shareholder wealth by mutual fund advisers. To judge whether such concern is warranted, the structure of investment companies over time must be explored.

Under a very broad definition, an investment company is any arrangement in which a number of persons invest in a *company*, which in turn invests in securities.[2]   While most investment companies are corporations, a minority are organized as trusts. Whether an investment company is a corporation or a trust has little significance for the economics

---

[2]Securities and Exchange Commission, "Public Policy Implications of Investment Company Growth," *Report of the Committee on Interstate and Foreign Commerce* (Washington D.C.:   U.S. Government Printing Office, December 2, 1966), 33.   [SEC, "Policy Implications"]

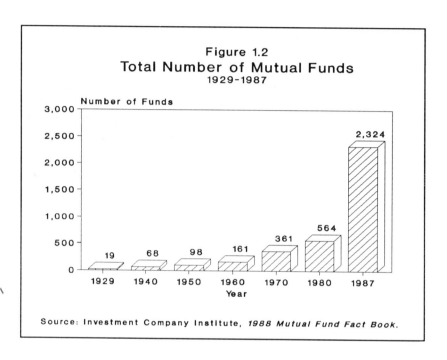

Figure 1.2
Total Number of Mutual Funds
1929-1987

Source: Investment Company Institute, *1988 Mutual Fund Fact Book*.

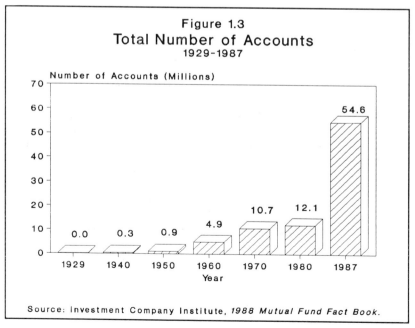

Figure 1.3
Total Number of Accounts
1929-1987

Source: Investment Company Institute, *1988 Mutual Fund Fact Book*.

of the industry, and the distinction will play no role in the discussion here.

Under the 1940 Act, registered investment companies are divided into three categories: (1) management companies; (2) face-amount certificate companies; and (3) unit investment trusts.[3]   All investment companies that are not specifically defined to fall into one of the latter two categories are automatically classified as management companies, which are the most common type of investment company.[4]

Management companies are classified into four categories based on a two-part test. The first part of the test is functional and depends on the degree of diversification in a company's investment portfolio.[5] The second part of the test is structural and depends on whether an investment company is open-end or closed-end.[6] Accordingly, the four categories of management companies are the following:

---

[3] SEC, "Policy Implications," 37.

[4] Face-amount certificate companies issue face-amount certificates that pay a fixed amount on maturity. Investors can purchase a certificate outright or through an installment payment plan. These certificates usually offer a lower rate than what is offered by federally insured savings institutions or U.S. Government securities. Unit investment trusts sell redeemable interests in units of specified securities. These companies can either hold one specific security or a number of securities. Changes in the composition of the underlying securities can be made only in predetermined contingencies. Investors can buy shares of an investment company on a periodic payment plan by purchasing them through a unit investment trust that invests solely in that investment company. See SEC, "Policy Implications," 37-38.

[5] An investment company is classified as diversified if, with respect to 75 percent of its total assets, not more than 5 percent of total assets is invested in a single company and not more than 10 percent of the outstanding shares of any one company are held in the portfolio. There are no investment restrictions on 25 percent of a diversified company's total assets. If a company cannot satisfy these criteria, then it is classified as a nondiversified company. See SEC, "Policy Implications," 39-40.

[6] SEC, "Policy Implications," 39.

1. Diversified, open-end
2. Nondiversified, open-end
3. Diversified, closed-end
4. Nondiversified, closed-end

The primary advantage of a diversified status derives from tax considerations. Provided that these companies distribute at least 90 percent of their pre-tax income, they are allowed to pass the pretax income on to shareholders, avoiding the double taxation to which most corporations are subject. Not surprisingly, the vast majority of investment companies are diversified.[7]

The difference between an open-end and closed-end investment company is structural. An open-end company, or mutual fund, offers shares continuously and is under a legal obligation to redeem shares at their net asset value (NAV). The NAV of a share is determined every day by dividing the value of the portfolio by the number of shares outstanding. Because of the continuous redemption feature of open-end funds, an open-end investment company must be prepared to distribute cash. Mutual funds therefore have a strong incentive to attract new shareholders to offset the cash outflow associated with redemptions.

Closed-end investment companies, however, are not obligated to redeem shares; rather, investors trade shares on the stock exchanges or in the over-the-counter market. While a closed-end company may issue shares continuously, most do not, since a new offering would dilute the interest of existing shareholders. Consequently, investment in a closed-end investment company is considerably less liquid than investment in mutual funds. In subsequent chapters we will examine how the distinctions between closed-end and open-end companies affect the nature of transactions between a fund's adviser and shareholders.

---

[7] Ibid., 41.

Mutual Funds

The most popular form of investment company today is the diversified open-end company or the mutual fund, which has been the major focus of contemporary litigation and regulatory initiatives.

Mutual funds are usually created by an investment adviser that remains closely affiliated with the fund. While a fund has a board of directors and executive officers, many of the directors and virtually all of the officers are employees of the advisory organization. However, under the 1940 Act, at least 40 percent of the directors must be unaffiliated with the investment adviser.

Mutual fund advisers perform various tasks on behalf of a fund's shareholders. They manage portfolio activities, which include conducting basic economic and financial research and making investment decisions for the assets in the fund's portfolio. In addition to portfolio management, the operation of an investment company requires several management and administrative services: (1) preparation, printing, and distribution of prospectuses, shareholder reports, and proxy materials; (2) holding of shareholder and directors' meetings; and (3) the issue, transfer, and cancellation of share certificates. Operation of a fund also requires activities related to the basic business of investing in assets, such as brokerage services, the safekeeping of assets, and the computation of offering and redemption prices for the fund's shares.

Mutual fund shareholders pay for the services of the fund's adviser through an advisory fee that is contractually established. This fee is commonly specified as some percentage of a fund's net assets and covers the costs of both management and nonmanagement services provided by the adviser. These costs generally include the costs of office space and support staff, as well as transfer and disbursement agent fees. Shareholders pay additional fees for those services not provided by the adviser, such as legal and auditing services and custodial services.[8]

In the majority of cases, a fund's adviser is part of the same organization that sponsors the mutual fund. Regulators fear that this feature, which makes it virtually impossible for a fund to sever its relationship with the adviser, enables advisers to take advantage of shareholders. The merits of such concerns will be evaluated more closely in subsequent chapters. Nevertheless, it is interesting to note that for a number of funds the advisory and administrative tasks are performed by separate organizations. Between 1982 and 1987, the percentage of total funds having separate advisers and administrators almost doubled, increasing from 6.6 to 12.7 percent (see Table 1.2).

In a majority of cases where services are obtained externally, either the adviser or administrator is part of a complex consisting of a very small number of mutual funds. Conversely, organizations that provide the full complement of services typically are large and consist of numerous funds. This pattern suggests that small organizations with few funds may be at a cost disadvantage relative to large complexes. The increase in the size of the typical complex over time may well have exacerbated the comparative disadvantages of a small organization.

As mentioned in the previous section, the distinguishing characteristic of a mutual fund is that its shareholders can redeem their shares from the investment company at any time they choose. Shares are purchased and redeemed at prices based on their net asset value, which in some cases is updated hourly. If a fund carries a sales load, this will be added to the net asset value of a share, and the purchase price will be greater than the value of the share. The sales load is a fee paid to the selling organization for its distribution efforts. Shares are usually redeemed at net asset value unless the fund carries a redemption fee, or back-end load.

---

[8] Ibid., 46.

Table 1.2

Number of Mutual Funds with Separate Adviser and Administrator
1982-1987

Year	Total number of funds	Funds with separate adviser and administrator	Percentage of total
1982	683	45	6.6
1983	850	70	8.2
1984	1,060	102	9.6
1985	1,262	144	11.4
1986	1,497	190	12.7
1987	1,764	224	12.7

Note: Data are as of 3/31 except for those of 1987, which are as of
12/31/86.
Source: Lipper — Directors' Analytical Data (May, 1982-1987).

Every mutual fund must have an explicitly stated objective, which is required by law to be explained in a fund's prospectus. An objective is a statement of the fund's investment goals and policies. Frequently, the objective will be a broad statement designed to give the fund's adviser discretion in pursuing a range of investment options. A typical objective reads: "The investment objective of [this fund] is long term capital appreciation through a diversified portfolio consisting primarily of common stocks in emerging growth companies and in special situations." [9]

A fund's objective acts as a guide for both investors and the fund's adviser. Mutual funds have a wide variety of different objectives, from money market mutual funds to

---

[9] Bull & Bear Capital Growth Fund, Inc. Prospectus (May 1, 1988), 1.

specialty funds that invest in only one industry.[10] An investor relies on a fund's announced objective for information about the riskiness of the underlying mutual fund portfolio. At the same time, fund advisers use a fund's objective as a boundary for their investment activity. Some fear that manipulation of a fund's investment activity without shareholder notification of a change in objective type is a potential area of abuse.

An investment company can distribute mutual fund shares to the public directly or through a sales force. Shares that are distributed through a sales force are available from brokers, financial planners, insurance agents, and sometimes through a special sales force contracted by the fund. These sales people are compensated for their efforts through a sales charge or load that is a fraction of the shares' NAV and is included in the share price. Funds that distribute shares directly are usually low-load or no-load,[11] though shareholders may pay explicit fees for direct distribution of shares if the fund's board of directors has approved a 12b-1 plan.[12]

There are three ways in which mutual fund shareholders can realize a return on their investment. First, a fund can distribute to shareholders the income and dividends earned on investments. Recall that a diversified fund is allowed to carry out these distributions on a pretax basis. Second, a fund can distribute any capital gains earned by the sale of securities. Finally, if the securities in the fund's portfolio increase in value, the NAV of a share will increase and an investor can realize a

---

[10] The funds in Fidelity's Select Portfolio Group are a good example of the latter. This group is comprised of 30 separate funds that restrict their investments to the securities of companies in specific industries, e.g., utilities, technology, and health care.

[11] Investment Company Institute, *1988 Mutual Fund Fact Book* (Washington, D.C., 1989), 7-8. [*1988 Mutual Fund Fact Book*]

[12] A 12b-1 fee pays for a fund's distribution costs such as advertising and printing or for commissions paid to brokers. The fee is named for the 1980 SEC rule permitting it. A fund's prospectus details 12b-1 charges, if applicable. See *1988 Mutual Fund Fact Book*, 57.

gain by redeeming shares. Investors have the option of having distributions automatically reinvested in additional shares of the fund, or receiving them directly in the form of a check.

Mutual funds frequently offer various services beyond automatic reinvestment of distributions. One such service is automatic withdrawal, in which a specified amount can be removed at regular intervals in the name of the shareholder or any individual the shareholder designates. Money market funds and other income funds often allow investors to make withdrawals by simply writing a check. Generally, checks on such funds must be over a minimum amount established by the fund, commonly $500. It should be noted, however, that some money market funds have no such limitations, and effectively function like checkable bank deposits. If an investor wishes to change investment objectives, most funds offer exchange privileges with other funds under common management. Finally, a shareholder's account activity is summarized on a periodic statement, which greatly facilitates record keeping.[13]

Money Market Mutual Funds

Money market mutual funds (MMFs) are of particular importance because they are fundamentally different from other types of mutual funds, and they account for a large portion of the assets currently invested in the industry. Money market funds are financial intermediaries that invest the pooled assets of many shareholders in a diversified portfolio of short-term money market instruments. Typical investment instruments include commercial paper, domestic commercial bank certificates of deposit, and U.S. treasury bills. The majority of MMFs are no-load. The actual rate of return realized by shareholders in MMFs is the net yield, or the difference between the fund's gross income and total expenses as a percentage of assets. In addition, depending on the way in

---

[13] *1988 Mutual Fund Fact Book*, 20-21.

which a fund is valued, its shareholders may or may not realize capital gains or losses.

Money market mutual funds were initially introduced by mutual fund advisers and stockbrokers in an attempt to retain investors. These funds encouraged the use of exchange features that allowed investors to switch from one type of investment vehicle to another. However, as documented below, the phenomenal growth of MMFs after 1977 stemmed from an opportunity created by the interest rate ceilings on deposits at banks and thrifts.

The two most common methods of valuing MMFs are (1) the amortized cost method and (2) the mark-to-market method. Under the amortized cost method, the value of the principal is unaffected by changes in market interest rates. Before the amortized cost method of valuation was declared acceptable, funds were required to value assets using the mark-to-market method. This method requires securities to be valued at their daily market values. Under amortized cost valuation, the yield on the MMF portfolio is a weighted moving average of past interest rates, which tend to be more stable than current interest rates. Because interest rate variations have no effect on the value of the assets, MMFs valued by the amortized cost method maintain a constant per-share asset value. In contrast, when MMF portfolios are valued by the mark-to-market method, shareholders may realize capital gains and losses in addition to the accrued interest.[14]

There are three general types of MMFs: (1) broker/ dealer funds, (2) general purpose funds, and (3) institutional funds. The main difference between the first two types of funds lies in the way in which shares are distributed. In the case of broker/dealer funds, the underwriter distributes fund shares through securities firms and their brokers. The brokers,

---

[14] For an analysis of share valuation techniques and, in particular, the possibility of arbitrage and shareholder dilution arising from the amortized cost method of valuation, see Andrew B. Lyon, "Money Market Funds and Shareholder Dilution," *The Journal of Finance*, vol. 39, no. 4 (September, 1984), 1101-1020.

in turn, deal directly with the public. Shares in general purpose funds, on the other hand, are purchased directly from the fund. General purpose funds offer their shares to investors through the mail, by telephone, bank wire, or possibly at their own retail offices. Individuals constitute the majority of investors in broker/dealer and general purpose funds.

Institutional funds specialize in serving businesses and bank trust departments. These funds typically are characterized by fewer investors and larger account sizes than their retail counterparts. At the end of 1987, only about 14 percent of all mutual fund accounts were held by institutions, even though institutions accounted for over 25 percent of total non-money market assets and nearly 50 percent of all money market assets. Table 1.3 and Figure 1.4 show the percentage of mutual fund industry assets attributed to institutional investors. Between 1954 and 1987, the percentage of total industry assets accounted for by institutional investors more than tripled, growing from 10.5 percent to 35.3 percent.

Fund Complexes

Mutual funds are typically organized by their advisers, which are often part of a larger corporate complex offering a range of financial intermediary and investment services. For example, a complex may consist of several mutual funds, a closed-end investment company, private investment counseling services, and brokerage activities. Each mutual fund in a complex is usually a separate legal entity. The funds are said to form a complex because each fund has a contract with the same adviser for investment management services.

Although mutual funds are legally organized as a series of individually operated companies, in practice, the majority of funds are little more than organizational pools with few, if any, employees other than officers and directors.[15] The actual job

---

[15] Donald W. Glazer, "A Study of Mutual Fund Complexes," *University of Pennsylvania Law Review*, vol. 119 (December, 1970), 205-282.

Table 1.3

Percentage of Mutual Fund Industry Assets Attributed to Institutional Investors
1954-1987

Year	Equity, bond, and income		Money market[a]		Total	
	Assets[b] ($ millions)	Percentage of total assets	Assets[b] ($ millions)	Percentage of total assets	Assets[b] ($ millions)	Percentage of total assets
1954	638.7	10.5%	--	--	638.7	10.5%
1956	841.6	9.3%	--	--	841.6	9.3%
1958	1,404.4	10.6%	--	--	1,404.4	10.6%
1960	2,015.6	11.8%	--	--	2,015.6	11.8%
1962	2,282.9	10.7%	--	--	2,282.9	10.7%
1964	3,262.5	11.2%	--	--	3,262.5	11.2%
1966	4,990.8	14.3%	--	--	4,990.8	14.3%
1968	7,827.0	14.9%	--	--	7,827.0	14.9%
1970	9,009.6	18.9%	--	--	9,009.6	18.9%
1972	11,922.8	19.9%	--	--	11,922.8	19.9%
1974	8,983.5	26.4%	NA	NA	NA	NA
1976	12,964.8	27.2%	NA	NA	NA	NA
1978	11,645.2	25.9%	NA	NA	NA	NA

continued on next page

Table 1.3 continued

	Equity, bond, and income		Money market[a]		Total	
Year	Assets[b] ($ millions)	Percentage of total assets	Assets[b] ($ millions)	Percentage of total assets	Assets[b] ($ millions)	Percentage of total assets
1980	16,405.7	28.1%	NA	NA	NA	NA
1981	13,081.3	23.7%	70,207.9	37.7%	83,289.2	34.5%
1982	17,792.6	23.2%	91,732.2	41.7%	109,524.8	36.9%
1983	25,986.5	22.9%	73,102.6	40.8%	99,089.1	33.8%
1984	32,742.9	23.9%	106,169.5	45.5%	138,912.4	37.5%
1985	61,870.3	24.6%	106,244.6	43.6%	168,114.9	33.9%
1986	116,964.9	27.6%	135,900.1	46.5%	252,865.0	35.3%
1987	121,725.2	26.8%	150,335.7	47.6%	272,060.9	35.3%

Notes: [a] Includes short-term municipal bond funds.
[b] Assets adjusted to estimate institutional share of nonreporting company assets.
NA = not available. Money market funds did not exist before 1974.

Source: Investment Company Institute, Mutual Fund Fact Book, 1984-1988 editions.

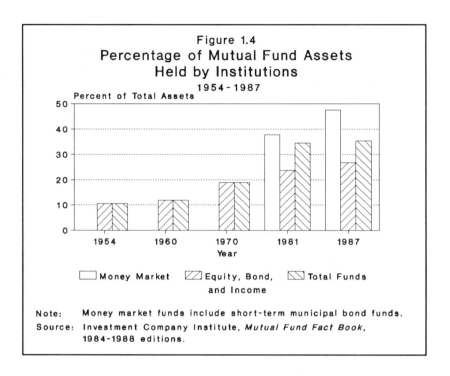

Figure 1.4
Percentage of Mutual Fund Assets
Held by Institutions
1954-1987

Note: Money market funds include short-term municipal bond funds.
Source: Investment Company Institute, *Mutual Fund Fact Book*,
         1984-1988 editions.

of running a fund is performed by the fund's adviser.[16]   The same adviser frequently serves a number of different mutual funds in a complex, or may serve funds in unaffiliated complexes.   In a minority of mutual fund complexes, the advisory function is contracted for externally.   These funds are free to replace the external adviser.   If the inability to replace a fund's adviser enabled the adviser to profit at the expense of shareholders, then vertical integration would be a means for advisers to extend their control over shareholders.[17]

---

[16] Mutual funds that are organized as trusts rather than as corporations are run by either the trustee named in the trust agreement or by an individual hired by the named trustee.

[17] The economics literature refers to this explanation as the domination theory.

Fund complexes are able to attract a wide range of investors with different risk preferences and investment objectives. In addition, investors frequently are permitted to switch to different funds in the complex at a reduced fee or no fee. As Table 1.4 shows, mutual fund complexes have assumed increased importance. By 1987, the average number of funds per complex had increased to 5.9. The number of funds offered by different complexes varies significantly. For example, in 1987, more than 10 percent of mutual fund complexes offered over 15 funds and one complex, Fidelity Management and Research Corp., offered over 100 funds.

Table 1.4

The Growth of Fund Complexes
1982-1987

Year	Number of funds	Number of complexes	Average number of funds per complex
1982	683	181	4.02
1983	850	215	4.28
1984	1,060	237	4.90
1985	1,262	270	5.21
1986	1,497	310	5.44
1987	1,764	338	5.88

Note: Figures are as of 3/31 except for those of 1987, which are as of 12/31/86. Average number of funds per complex is not equal to the number of funds divided by the number of complexes because in cases where the fund has a separate adviser and administrator, funds are part of more than one complex (see Table 1.2 for number of funds with separate adviser and administrator).

Source: Lipper — Director's Analytical Data (Spring, 1982-1987).

PRE-1940

Early investment companies differed considerably from today's investment companies. However, many of the initial characteristics of investment companies proved important in eliciting the first regulatory actions affecting the mutual fund industry.

The origin of investment companies can be traced back to money borrowed from British investment companies to finance post-Civil War industrial expansion. As the United States economy grew, investment companies were formed in Boston, Philadelphia, and New York. The earliest investment companies were small and lacked uniform structures. Frequently, they were formed to avoid taxes or regulations.

In 1924, the first major closed-end and open-end companies were formed. Dillon, Read & Co. offered the first closed-end company with publicly traded shares, the U.S. & Foreign Securities Corporation (U.S. & Foreign). Massachusetts Investors Trust (MIT) was the first open-end, or mutual fund, company. By the end of 1924, MIT had 200 shareholders holding 32,296 shares with a total asset value of $392,000.

Over the next three years, 56 new closed-end funds and 13 new open-end funds were started. However, the industry was still small and concentrated by today's standards. Before the stock market crash in 1929, closed-end funds dominated the industry. In 1929, there were 89 closed-end funds, which held 95.4 percent of all investment company assets, with a total of $2.89 billion invested by 533,000 shareholders. By comparison, there were only 19 open-end funds with a total of $0.14 billion invested by 49,000 shareholders.

Table 1.5 illustrates the change in popularity of closed-end funds compared to open-end funds. Closed-end funds are difficult to liquidate, especially during a crisis of the magnitude of the stock market crash. While open-end funds also declined in value as a result of the crash, they experienced rapid growth in the 1930s as investors switched from closed-end funds. In 1929, about $100 million was invested in open-end companies. By 1940, open-end assets had grown to nearly $500 million and

Table 1.5

Total Investment Company Assets by Company Type
1929-1987

Year	Closed-end ($ billions)	Open-end ($ billions)	Total ($ billions)	Closed-end as percentage of total
1929	2.9	0.1	3.0	95.4%
1940	0.6	0.5	1.1	57.5%
1950	0.9	2.5	3.4	25.8%
1960	2.1	17.0	19.1	10.9%
1970	4.0	47.6	51.6	7.8%
1980	7.9	134.8	142.7	5.5%
1987	20.5	769.9	790.4	2.6%

Source: "The Mutual Fund Industry: A Legal Survey," Notre Dame Lawyer, vol. 44 (1968-1969), 782; Wiesenberger Financial Services, Investment Companies (1976); Investment Company Institute, 1988 Mutual Fund Fact Book.

the percent of management company assets invested in closed-end funds had declined to 57.5.

1940 TO 1970

Mutual funds grew substantially in the 30 years from 1940 to 1970, with assets averaging nearly 17 percent growth per year (see Table 1.6). This growth was achieved through both (1) capital appreciation of assets already invested in funds and (2) positive net sales of fund shares. Mutual funds provided small investors with an opportunity to invest in a diversified portfolio managed by a professional money manager. A majority of funds in this period were equity-oriented. However, a small number of bond funds provided an alternative to traditional equity investments.

Table 1.6

Mutual Fund Industry Totals
1940-1970

Year	Total assets ($ thousands)	Total number of funds	Total number of accounts
1940	447,959	68	296,056
1941	401,611	68	293,251
1942	486,850	68	312,609
1943	653,653	68	341,435
1944	882,191	68	421,675
1945	1,284,185	73	497,875
1946	1,311,108	74	580,221
1947	1,409,165	80	672,543
1948	1,505,762	87	722,118
1949	1,973,547	91	842,198
1950	2,530,563	98	938,651
1951	3,129,629	103	1,110,432
1952	3,931,407	110	1,359,000
1953	4,146,061	110	1,537,250
1954	6,109,390	115	1,703,846
1955	7,837,524	125	2,085,325
1956	9,046,431	135	2,580,049
1957	8,714,143	143	3,110,392
1958	13,242,388	151	3,630,096
1959	15,817,962	155	4,276,077
1960	17,025,684	161	4,897,600
1961	22,788,812	170	5,319,201
1962	21,270,735	169	5,910,455
1963	25,214,436	165	6,151,935
1964	29,116,254	160	6,301,908
1965	35,220,243	170	6,709,343
1966	34,829,353	182	7,701,656
1967	44,701,302	204	7,904,132
1968	52,677,188	240	9,080,168
1969	48,290,733	269	10,166,788
1970	47,618,100	361	10,690,312
Average annual growth	16.8%	5.7%	12.7%

Source: Investment Company Institute, Mutual Fund Fact Book, 1984-1988 editions, and Trends in Mutual Fund Activity (March, 1985).

Table 1.7 presents information on annual sales and redemptions of mutual fund assets. The value of mutual fund assets fluctuates as a result both of net sales and of changes in

Table 1.7

Mutual Fund Sales, Redemptions, and Assets
1941-1970

Year	Sales ($ millions)	Redemptions ($ millions)	Net sales[a] ($ millions)	Assets ($ millions)
1941	53.3	45.0	8.3	401.6
1942	73.1	25.4	47.7	486.9
1943	116.1	51.2	64.8	653.7
1944	169.2	70.8	98.4	882.2
1945	292.4	110.0	182.4	1,284.2
1946	370.4	143.6	226.7	1,311.1
1947	266.9	88.7	178.2	1,409.2
1948	273.8	127.2	146.6	1,505.8
1949	385.5	107.6	277.9	1,973.5
1950	518.8	280.7	238.1	2,530.6
1951	674.6	321.6	353.1	3,129.6
1952	782.9	196.0	586.9	3,931.4
1953	672.0	238.8	433.2	4,146.1
1954	862.8	399.7	463.1	6,109.4
1955	1,207.5	442.6	764.9	7,837.5
1956	1,346.7	432.8	914.0	9,046.4
1957	1,390.6	405.7	984.8	8,714.1
1958	1,619.8	511.3	1,108.5	13,242.4
1959	2,280.0	785.6	1,494.4	15,818.0
1960	2,097.2	841.8	1,255.4	17,025.7
1961	2,950.9	1,160.4	1,790.5	22,788.8
1962	2,699.0	1,122.7	1,576.4	21,270.7
1963	2,459.1	1,505.3	953.8	25,214.4
1964	3,403.0	1,874.1	1,528.9	29,116.3
1965	4,358.1	1,962.4	2,395.7	35,220.2
1966	4,671.8	2,005.1	2,666.8	34,829.4
1967	4,699.6	2,744.2	1,955.4	44,701.3
1968	6,819.8	3,838.7	2,981.1	52,677.2
1969	6,718.3	3,661.6	3,056.6	48,290.7
1970	4,625.8	2,987.6	1,638.2	47,618.1

Note: [a] Net sales is equal to sales minus redemptions.
Source: Investment Company Institute, Mutual Fund Fact Book, 1984-1988
        editions, and Trends in Mutual Fund Activity (March, 1985).

the net asset value per share. For example, during the period between 1952 and 1958, total net sales accounted for approximately 50 percent of the $9.3 billion in asset growth, while the remaining 50 percent is attributable to an increase in the market value of the underlying securities in the portfolio of mutual funds.

Table 1.6 provides information on the total number of shareholder accounts. The number of shareholders increased from about 0.3 million in 1940 to 10.7 million in 1970. This increase represents an average annual growth of approximately 13 percent. Over this period, the average account size tripled in nominal terms. In 1970, average assets per account were $4,500, compared to $1,500 in 1940. In real terms, however, average account size remained remarkably stable and actually declined slightly. When expressed in constant 1987 dollars, the average account size in 1940 was $13,816, and fell to $12,589 in 1970.

Not only did mutual fund assets increase rapidly in size during this period, but also the number of mutual funds expanded significantly, rising from 68 in 1940 to 361 in 1970, an average annual increase of about six percent (see Table 1.6). The growth in the number of funds has direct implications for an evaluation of the appropriateness of regulatory measures affecting the mutual fund industry, since the growth is an indicator of the competitiveness of the market. This will be explored in greater depth in Chapter Five.

1970 TO THE PRESENT

Overview

While average annual industry growth of assets in the post-1970 period was comparable to the growth rate between 1940 and 1970, there have been fundamental shifts in the underlying structure of the industry. Industry growth is no longer attributable to investment in traditional equity-oriented funds, but rather to investment in a variety of new fund types. Table 1.8 presents information on mutual fund assets, funds, and accounts in the period between 1970 and 1987.

Volatile stock market conditions and increased inflation in the early 1970s reduced the relative attractiveness of traditional mutual funds and by 1974 total assets had fallen substantially. In an attempt to retain investors, mutual fund advisers and stockbrokers in 1974 introduced a new fund type, the MMF. Since the late 1970s, the offering of new types of funds has contributed significantly to steady growth in the industry. Following the success of MMFs, advisers introduced the first municipal bond fund in 1976, the first option-income fund in 1977, and the first government income and Ginnie Mae funds in the early 1980s.[18] The proliferation of new fund types has given increased importance to fund complexes. The industry, which was characterized by individual equity-oriented funds, has evolved into a diversified financial industry able to respond to changing market conditions and investor demands.

Money Market Mutual Funds

Between 1974 and 1977, assets invested in MMFs increased only slightly, from $1.7 billion to $3.9 billion (see Table 1.8). However, beginning in 1978 and continuing through 1982, investment in MMFs accelerated, peaking in 1981. Between 1982 and 1985, assets invested in MMFs remained fairly constant; in 1987, they increased to an all-time peak of $316.1 billion.

Much of the initial growth in MMFs occurred as a result of the demand created by consumers with savings in passbook accounts. Deposit rate ceilings under Regulation Q and other liability requirements prevented traditional financial intermediaries from offering a liquid deposit account that yielded a rate of interest as high as the market rate. Table 1.9 shows the average annual return between 1975 and 1987 for the

---

[18] *1988 Mutual Fund Fact Book*, 11.

Table 1.8

Mutual Fund Industry Totals
1970-1987

	Total assets ($ thousands)			Total number of funds			Total number of accounts		
Year	Equity, bond, and income	Money market	Total	Equity, bond, and income	Money market	Total	Equity, bond, and income	Money market	Total
1970	47,618,100	-	47,618,100	361	-	361	10,690,312	-	10,690,312
1971	55,045,328	-	55,045,328	392	-	392	10,900,952	-	10,900,952
1972	59,830,646	-	59,830,646	410	-	410	10,635,287	-	10,635,287
1973	46,518,535	-	46,518,535	421	-	421	10,330,862	-	10,330,862
1974	34,061,746	1,715,100	35,776,846	416	15	431	9,970,439	-	9,970,439
1975	42,178,683	3,695,700	45,874,383	390	36	426	9,667,305	208,777	9,876,082
1976	47,581,812	3,685,800	51,267,612	404	48	452	8,879,413	180,676	9,060,089
1977	45,149,151	3,887,700	49,036,851	427	50	477	8,515,079	177,522	8,692,601
1978	44,979,685	10,858,000	55,837,685	444	61	505	8,190,551	467,803	8,658,354
1979	48,979,431	45,214,200	94,193,631	446	76	522	7,482,166	2,307,852	9,790,018

continued on next page

Table 1.8 continued

Year	Total assets ($ thousands)			Total number of funds			Total number of accounts		
	Equity, bond, and income	Money market	Total	Equity, bond, and income	Money market	Total	Equity, bond, and income	Money market	Total
1980	58,399,621	76,361,300	134,760,921	458	106	564	7,325,543	4,762,103	12,087,646
1981	55,207,308	186,158,200	241,365,508	486	179	665	7,175,472	10,323,466	17,498,938
1982	76,840,624	219,837,500	296,678,124	539	318	857	8,190,266	13,258,143	21,448,409
1983	113,598,564	179,386,500	292,985,064	653	373	1,026	12,064,971	12,539,688	24,604,659
1984	137,126,206	233,553,800	370,680,006	820	426	1,246	14,423,644	13,844,697	28,268,341
1985	251,695,070	243,802,400	495,497,470	1,071	460	1,531	19,845,558	14,954,726	34,800,284
1986	424,156,400	292,151,600	716,308,000	1,356	487	1,843	29,790,000	16,313,148	46,103,148
1987	453,842,400	316,096,100	769,938,500	1,781	543	2,324	36,971,000	17,674,790	54,645,790
Avg. Annual Growth	14.2%	49.4%	17.8%	9.8%	31.8%	11.6%	7.6%	44.8%	10.1%

Note: **Money market** includes both money market and short-term municipal bond funds.
Source: Investment Company Institute, <u>Mutual Fund Fact Book</u> (1984-1988).

Table 1.9

Average Annual Return by Investment Instrument
1975-1987

Year	Money market mutual funds	Three-month Treasury bills	Passbook accounts	Money market deposit accounts
1975	6.17%	5.84%	5.25%	-
1976	5.20%	4.99%	5.25%	-
1977	4.86%	5.27%	5.25%	-
1978	7.02%	7.22%	5.25%	-
1979	10.27%	10.04%	5.50%	-
1980	12.06%	11.51%	5.50%	-
1981	16.84%	14.03%	5.50%	-
1982	12.22%	10.69%	5.50%	10.38%
1983	8.53%	8.63%	5.50%	8.51%
1984	9.98%	9.58%	5.50%	9.28%
1985	7.65%	7.48%	5.50%	7.35%
1986	6.20%	5.98%	5.50%	5.84%
1987	6.01%	5.82%	5.19%	5.25%

Sources: Donoghue's Money Fund Report (December, 1977-1988); Butler's Money Fund Report (December, 1975-1976); 1988 Economic Report of the President; Bank Rate Monitor; Federal Reserve Statistical Release: H-6.

following investment instruments, all offering low risk and high liquidity: MMFs, three-month treasury bills, passbook savings accounts, and money market deposit accounts (MMDAs). As short-term interest rates continued to rise, the difference between (1) the deposit rate ceiling of 5.5 percent and (2) the average net yield on relatively safe and highly liquid MMFs grew to 11.3 percent in 1981. In the same year, the predictably dramatic net increase in MMF assets was 144 percent. The relationship between the gap in interest rates and the growth in MMF assets is described in Figure 1.5, which plots the year-to-year change in MMF assets against the interest rate differential between MMFs and MMDAs and MMFs and passbook savings, both measures of opportunity cost, for each year between 1978 and 1987. While the relationship between the change in MMF assets and interest rate differences is far

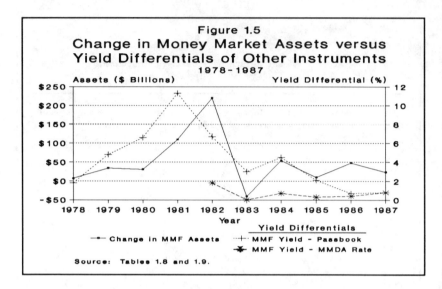

Figure 1.5
Change in Money Market Assets versus
Yield Differentials of Other Instruments
1978-1987

Source: Tables 1.8 and 1.9.

from perfect, the relative return offered by MMFs clearly influenced the level of investment in these assets.

Before the MMFs arose, money market investment was beyond the means of most small investors because money market instruments often have minimum denominations in excess of $10,000. MMFs, most of which required only a minimal investment, gave small investors the opportunity to realize money market returns that were five to ten percentage points, or from 100 percent to 200 percent greater, than the 5.5 percent rate paid on passbook savings accounts.

The rapid rise of MMFs can be viewed as a classic example of financial market innovation and the free market's ability to circumvent regulation. Had the traditional depository intermediaries, e.g., commercial banks and thrifts, been deregulated, the option of fully insured deposit accounts offering market interest rates undoubtedly would have limited the appeal of MMFs. In fact, as discussed below, the effect of the introduction of MMDAs on the demand for MMFs supports this conclusion.

The inability of commercial banks and thrifts to compete for the savings dollars of consumers led to financial disintermediation as savings in these institutions were redirected into MMFs. Table 1.10 shows both the total assets and the annual percent change in assets invested in MMFs, savings deposits, and MMDAs between 1977 and 1987. From 1977 to 1982, there was a striking contrast in the behavior of savings deposits, which declined by $125 billion, and assets invested in MMFs, which grew by more than $200 billion.

One of the most significant influences on the subsequent development of MMFs has been that of increased competition. This competition had already begun in 1978 when thrift institutions and commercial banks were for the first time permitted to offer money market certificates. Competition was further enhanced in 1981 by legislation that permitted banks and thrifts to offer NOW accounts. The most significant increase in the ability of banks and thrifts to compete with MMFs was the further deregulation of the banking industry that allowed banks and thrifts to offer MMDAs.

As a result of this legislation, banks and thrifts were permitted to offer rates competitive with those of the MMFs. The virtual disappearance of the differential between (1) the interest that could be earned on bank and thrift deposit accounts and (2) the net yield on MMFs has had a substantial influence on the growth of the MMFs. Whereas in 1981 that differential (relative to passbook accounts) was greater than 11 percent, in 1985 the differential between (1) the average net yield of 7.65 percent offered by MMFs and (2) the average net yield of 7.30 percent offered by MMDAs was a mere 35 basis points. Between 1982 and 1987, assets invested in MMDAs grew from $42.9 billion to $525.2 billion (see Table 1.10). At the same time, assets invested in MMFs fell from their 1982 peak of $219.8 billion to $179.4 billion in 1983, although thereafter they resumed their growth, rising to $316.1 billion in 1987.[19]

---

[19] Money market deposit accounts also compete with MMFs in the area of check-writing privileges. Since the introduction of MMDAs, many MMFs have lowered their minimum check withdrawal amounts. See Donoghue Organization, Inc., *Donoghue's Mutual Fund Almanac*, 1983-1988 editions.

Table 1.10

Annual Change in Total Assets Invested
1977-1987

Year	Money market mutual funds		Savings deposits		Money market deposit accounts	
	Total assets ($ billions)	Percentage change	Total assets ($ billions)	Percentage change	Total assets ($ billions)	Percentage change
1977	3.9	-	483.1	-	-	-
1978	10.9	179.49	478.0	-1.06	-	-
1979	45.2	314.68	420.7	-11.99	-	-
1980	76.4	69.03	398.3	-5.32	-	-
1981	186.2	143.72	342.2	-14.08	-	-
1982	219.8	18.05	357.6	4.50	42.9	-
1983	179.4	-18.38	308.5	-13.73	375.9	776.22
1984	233.6	30.21	287.9	-6.68	416.9	10.91
1985	243.8	4.37	301.8	4.83	512.0	22.81
1986	292.2	19.85	370.7	22.83	572.5	11.82
1987	316.1	8.18	414.2	11.73	525.2	-8.26

Note: Money market mutual funds include short-term municipal bond funds.
Source: Investment Company Institute, 1988 Mutual Fund Fact Book; Federal Reserve Bank Bulletin.

Aside from the competition from banks and thrifts, there was one other notable influence upon the evolution of MMFs in the 1980s. The general decline in the level of short-term interest rates in conjunction with the rejuvenation of the stock market has presumably caused a number of investors to divert their assets away from money market funds into equity investments and long-term bonds. The average yield on MMFs fell from 16.84 percent in 1981 to 6.01 percent in 1987. The effect this decline has had on the relative demand for MMFs can be seen in Table 1.11, which shows the share of assets of MMFs compared to those of non-MMFs. Between 1974 and 1981, MMFs accounted for an increasing share of the growing mutual fund assets. However, between 1981 and 1987, the relative share of MMFs declined. By 1987, only 41 percent of mutual fund assets were invested in MMFs compared to 77 percent at their peak in 1981.

Table 1.11

Share of All Mutual Fund Assets: Money Market Versus Other Mutual Funds
1974-1987

Year	Equity, bond, and income	Money market	Total assets ($ billions)
1974	95.2%	4.8%	35.8
1975	91.9%	8.1%	45.9
1976	92.8%	7.2%	51.3
1977	92.1%	7.9%	49.0
1978	80.6%	19.4%	55.8
1979	52.0%	48.0%	94.2
1980	43.3%	56.7%	134.8
1981	22.9%	77.1%	241.4
1982	25.9%	74.1%	296.7
1983	38.8%	61.2%	293.0
1984	37.0%	63.0%	370.7
1985	50.8%	49.2%	495.5
1986	59.2%	40.8%	716.3
1987	58.9%	41.1%	769.9

Note: **Money market** includes short-term municipal bond funds.
Source: Investment Company Institute, Mutual Fund Fact Book, 1984-1988 editions.

In an attempt to attract new investors, fund advisers continually segmented the industry, offering an increasing number of fund types. In 1975, the mutual fund industry offered investors seven investment objectives; by the end of 1987, these objectives had been segmented into 22 different categories. These different types of objective are described in Table 1.12, which shows the distribution of the number of funds by investment objective for the years 1980 through 1987. While in 1980, growth funds accounted for a greater fraction of all funds than did MMFs, MMFs have been the most common fund type in every year since, followed by the traditional growth fund. Although there are more MMFs than any other type of fund, their popularity has decreased somewhat in recent years. In 1982, money market funds accounted for a third of all funds; by 1987, MMFs represented only 17 percent of all funds.

Other Mutual Funds

As just noted, equity, bond, and income funds exhibited little growth until the stock market rally of the 1980s. Total assets invested in these three types of funds increased by approximately 15 percent between 1970 and 1981 (see Table 1.8). However, by the end of 1987, total assets had increased to $453.8 billion, resulting in an average annual growth rate of over 40 percent between 1981 and 1987. The number of shareholder accounts increased at a average annual rate of approximately 30 percent in this six-year period.

Table 1.13 presents the distribution of mutual fund assets by investment objective. While a plethora of investment objectives is available, in 1980 the top three investment objectives alone — money market, growth, and growth income — accounted for over 80 percent of total mutual fund assets. By 1987, a number of investment objectives had gained substantial popularity, including government income and long-term and short-term municipal bonds. Clearly, growth in the mutual fund industry during the 1980s was fueled by the performance of the

Table 1.12

Percentage of Mutual Funds by Investment Objective
1980-1987

Percentage of total by year

Objective	1980	1981	1982	1983	1984	1985	1986	1987
Aggressive growth	9.4	9.3	9.2	9.2	9.7	9.2	8.7	8.0
Growth	24.3	21.8	18.1	16.8	16.9	14.0	14.1	13.3
Precious metal	-	-	-	-	-	1.1	1.2	0.9
International	-	-	-	-	-	2.5	3.2	2.0
Global equity	-	-	-	-	-	-	-	1.5
Growth and income	13.7	11.9	10.0	10.5	9.6	9.9	9.6	8.1
Balanced	3.7	3.0	2.3	2.1	1.7	1.6	1.5	1.3
Flexible portfolio	-	-	-	-	-	-	-	1.2
Income - mixed	9.9	8.6	7.7	8.3	10.1	5.4	6.2	3.8
Income - equity	-	-	-	-	-	-	-	1.9
Income - bond	-	-	-	-	-	-	-	3.8
Option/income	1.8	1.5	1.1	1.2	1.1	1.1	1.1	0.8
U.S. Government income	-	-	-	-	-	3.5	5.2	6.4
Corporate bond	11.0	10.1	8.6	8.0	7.5	8.1	6.9	1.8
Global bond	-	-	-	-	-	-	-	0.7

continued on next page

Table 1.12 continued

				Percentage of total by year				
Objective	1980	1981	1982	1983	1984	1985	1986	1987
High-yield bond	-	-	-	-	-	-	-	3.0
Ginnie Mae	-	-	-	-	-	2.2	2.4	2.4
Long-term national municipal bond	7.4	6.9	5.8	7.6	9.1	6.6	6.8	6.5
Long-term state municipal bond	-	-	-	-	-	4.8	6.6	9.4
Short-term national municipal bond	1.8	3.0	4.3	6.4	7.8	7.3	6.9	4.8
Short-term state municipal bond	-	-	-	-	-	-	-	1.8
Money market	17.0	23.9	32.8	29.9	26.4	22.7	19.5	16.7
Total number of funds	564	665	857	1,026	1,246	1,531	1,843	2,324
Total number of objective types	10	10	10	10	10	15	15	22

Source: Investment Company Institute, Mutual Fund Fact Book, 1984-1988 editions.

Table 1.13

Mutual Fund Total Assets by Investment Objective
1980-1987

Objective				Percentage of total by year				
	1980	1981	1982	1983	1984	1985	1986	1987
Aggressive growth	3.5	2.1	3.2	6.4	3.8	4.1	3.5	3.5
Growth	12.5	6.3	6.4	8.9	7.2	7.1	6.1	6.2
Precious metal	-	-	-	-	0.1	0.3	0.3	0.5
International	-	-	-	-	1.4	1.6	1.0	0.9
Global equity	-	-	-	-	-	-	1.2	1.4
Growth and income	14.5	7.5	7.4	10.0	8.5	9.1	7.8	8.3
Balanced	2.5	1.2	1.0	1.1	0.8	0.8	1.0	1.2
Flexible portfolio	-	-	-	-	-	-	-	0.6
Income - mixed	3.6	1.9	2.0	3.0	1.9	2.2	1.4	1.5
Income - equity	-	-	-	-	-	-	1.8	1.9
Income - bond	-	-	-	-	-	-	1.6	1.6
Option/income	0.4	0.2	0.3	0.6	0.9	1.1	1.0	0.7
U.S. Government income	-	-	-	-	1.7	8.1	11.5	11.5
Corporate bond	4.2	2.4	3.1	3.9	3.9	4.8	1.3	1.2
Global bond	-	-	-	-	-	-	0.1	0.3
High-yield bond	-	-	-	-	-	-	3.4	3.1
Ginnie Mae	-	-	-	-	1.1	3.6	5.5	4.4

continued on next page

Table 1.13 continued

Objective	1980	1981	1982	1983	1984	Percentage of total by year 1985	1986	1987
Long-term national municipal bond	2.2	1.3	2.5	5.0	4.3	5.6	7.0	6.4
Long-term state municipal bond	-	-	-	-	1.3	2.3	3.6	3.6
Short-term national municipal bond	1.4	1.7	4.4	5.7	6.4	7.3	8.3	7.1
Short-term state municipal bond	-	-	-	-	-	-	0.6	0.9
Money market	55.2	75.4	69.6	55.5	56.6	41.9	31.9	33.1
Total assets ($ billions)	134.8	241.4	296.7	293.0	370.7	495.5	716.3	769.9

Note: The data presented here are not necessarily consistent with those of Table 1.12 due to subsequent reclassifications of fund objectives in the following year. In contrast, Table 1.12 presents data that are not reclassified afterwards according to the following year's categories.

Source: Investment Company Institute, Mutual Fund Fact Book, 1984-1988 editions.

stock market and the simultaneous segmentation of the mutual fund industry in pursuit of new investors.

Another significant development after 1970 has been the reduction or elimination of sales loads. The significance of sales loads stems from their effect on investor mobility. Sales loads tend to reduce investor mobility by increasing the transaction costs of share purchases and redemptions. Table 1.14 shows mutual fund assets invested in load versus no-load funds. In 1970, almost 95 percent of total mutual fund assets were invested in load funds, with typical sales loads ranging from 7.50 to 8.75 percent. However, both no-load and low-load funds increased in popularity, with sales loads charged by low-load funds falling as low as 4 percent. In 1983, 73 percent of all mutual fund assets were invested in no-load funds. No-load funds of every investment objective are now available to investors. The reduction or removal of loads has reduced the

Table 1.14

Mutual Fund Assets: Load Versus No-Load
1970-1983

Year	Load assets ($ millions)	Percentage of total	No-load assets ($ millions)	Percentage of total	Total assets ($ millions)
1970	44,858.8	94.2%	2,759.3	5.8%	47,618.1
1971	51,035.3	92.7%	4,010.0	7.3%	55,045.3
1972	53,907.1	90.1%	5,923.5	9.9%	59,830.6
1973	41,632.7	89.5%	4,885.8	10.5%	46,518.5
1974	30,508.7	85.3%	5,268.1	14.7%	35,776.8
1975	37,577.1	81.9%	8,297.3	18.1%	45,874.4
1976	41,455.7	80.9%	9,811.9	19.1%	51,267.6
1977	36,284.4	74.1%	12,652.5	25.9%	48,936.9
1978	35,572.3	63.7%	20,265.4	36.3%	55,837.7
1979	36,249.9	38.4%	58,261.4	61.6%	94,511.3
1980	42,995.4	31.9%	91,765.5	68.1%	134,760.9
1981	40,923.5	17.0%	200,441.9	83.0%	241,365.4
1982	55,270.6	18.6%	241,407.5	81.4%	296,678.1
1983	79,808.6	27.2%	213,176.5	72.8%	292,985.1

Source: Investment Company Institute, Mutual Fund Fact Book, 1984-1988 ediitons.

costs associated with mutual fund transactions, which is a critical factor in increasing investor mobility.

CONCLUSIONS

Mutual funds have evolved as a reaction to market conditions. This evolution was particularly clear in the case of MMFs, but is true more generally as well. The growth of mutual fund complexes that provide several funds with different objectives under one corporate umbrella has provided investors a wide variety of investment opportunities. The provision of new attributes that are valuable to investors has been a notable characteristic of the evolution of the mutual fund industry. A detailed analysis of the way in which the changes discussed in this chapter have affected the underlying competitiveness of mutual funds will be offered in later chapters.

The mutual fund industry has undergone numerous changes since its inception. For policy purposes, it is important that current regulations affecting mutual funds reflect the current state of market conditions; otherwise, significant distortions and inefficiencies may result. A thorough analysis of current regulations in light of the changes in the mutual fund industry will determine whether mutual funds, and, in particular, the fees charged by fund advisers, require policing, or, whether the structure of the mutual fund market is sufficiently competitive to prevent the types of abuses that current regulations were designed to curtail.

TWO

REGULATION OF THE MUTUAL FUND INDUSTRY

BACKGROUND

One of the primary objectives of the Investment Company Act of 1940 was to protect small investors in mutual funds against abuses by a fund's adviser. Proponents of mutual fund regulation believed that, because of the inability of investors to replace a fund's adviser with a new adviser should the adviser charge excessive fees or otherwise take advantage of a fund's shareholders, the usual bargaining that is part of the competitive process is absent from the adviser-shareholder relationship. This sentiment is articulated in the following language of the Senate:

> Since a typical fund is organized by its investment adviser which provides it with almost all management services and because its shares are bought by investors who rely on that service, a mutual fund cannot, as a practical matter, sever its relationship with the adviser. Therefore, the forces of arm's length bargaining do not work in the mutual fund industry in the same manner as they do in other sectors of the American economy.[20]

The Investment Company Act of 1940 embodies most of the regulatory guidelines controlling the mutual fund industry.

---

[20] "Investment Company Amendments Act of 1970," *Senate Report* No. 91-184, 91st Congress, 2d Session (1970). [*Senate Report*]

In the 1960s Congress ordered an extensive re-evaluation of the mutual fund industry, which resulted in the 1970 Amendments to the 1940 Act. The 1970 Amendments increased the scope of regulation with respect to the fiduciary duties of mutual fund advisers and to criteria for selecting a fund's board of directors. Since 1970, the SEC has offered several proposals for modification of the Investment Company Act of 1940. While the SEC has adopted new rules and amendments to the 1940 Act, the basic content of the Act remains substantially unchanged.

INVESTMENT COMPANY ACT OF 1940

Purpose of the Act

In 1939 the SEC submitted to Congress an extensive study of the investment trust and investment company industry.[21] Among other things, the SEC study found many instances of self-seeking behavior by mutual fund providers with disregard for the interests of shareholders. It has been estimated that the amount of investors' wealth effectively expropriated by mutual fund providers amounted to $1.1 billion during the 1920s and 1930s.[22] To minimize the likelihood that future expropriations would occur, the study called for regulation beyond that instituted in the Securities Act of 1933 and the Securities Exchange Act of 1934. This led to the Investment Company Act of 1940.[23]

---

[21] The study, designated the "Report of the Securities and Exchange Commission on Investment Trusts and Investment Companies," was produced in five parts totaling 33,000 pages and 4,800 exhibits and was submitted to Congress over three years.

[22] "The Mutual Fund Industry: A Legal Survey," *Notre Dame Lawyer*, vol. 44 (1968-1969), 781.

[23] Ibid., 794.

The Act deals with eight particular issues: [24]

1. Inadequate disclosure of relevant information to purchasers of securities issued by investment companies
2. The organization or management of investment companies leading to pursuit of the interest of the company or affiliated persons rather than the interest of the shareholders
3. The issue of securities in a manner that is inequitable or discriminatory, or fails to protect the privileges to which current shareholders are entitled
4. Mismanagement of investment companies by irresponsible persons or concentration of control through pyramiding or other inequitable methods
5. Unsound or misleading accounting practices of investment companies that are not subject to independent review
6. Restructuring of an investment company without approval of the shareholders
7. Excessive borrowing and issue of excessive amounts of senior debt, which increase the speculative character of junior securities
8. Operation of investment companies without adequate assets or reserves

Advisers of management companies employed a variety of tactics that apparently permitted them to expropriate shareholder wealth or to leverage their corporate control. One scheme, referred to as pyramiding, was a technique used to extend the control of the investment adviser. The following example involving Dillon, Read & Co. describes an actual pyramiding scheme.

The U.S. & Foreign Securities Corporation (U.S. & Foreign), the first major closed-end investment company, was formed by Dillon, Read & Co. by issuing three classes of securities: (1) $25 million of no-par first preferred, (2) $5 million of no-par second preferred, and (3) one million shares

---

[24] *Investment Company Act of 1940*, sec. 80a-1(b). [*ICA of 1940*]

of no-par common stock. The first preferred was sold to the
public, with 250,000 shares of the common stock attached as a
bonus. Dillon, Read purchased all of the second preferred,
which carried the right to the remaining 750,000 shares of
common stock. Dillon, Read was able to extend its control
even further by forming a second investment company, the U.S.
& International Securities Corporation (U.S. & International),
which had a capital structure similar to that of U.S. & Foreign.
A total of $50 million in first preferred was issued to the
public, which also received 500,000 shares of common stock and
warrants for an additional 500,000 shares of common stock.
U.S. & Foreign purchased $10 million in second preferred,
which was accompanied by 2 million shares of common stock.
Therefore, through pyramiding of investment companies,
Dillon, Read effectively controlled two funds with equity
totalling $80 million with an investment of only $5 million.[25]

The significance of such a pyramiding scheme rests in its
effect on public shareholders. To the extent that such schemes
permit advisers like Dillon, Read to generate private benefits
for themselves at the expense of shareholders who lack control,
there is a transfer of wealth from shareholders to a fund's
adviser. However, such wealth transfers are limited by (1) the
ability of public shareholders to monitor the adviser's behavior
and (2) the competitive pressure that requires shareholders to
receive yields that match current competitive standards.
However, the self-dealing transactions described below suggest
that at least the first protective constraint, effective monitoring
by shareholders, was largely absent in the 1920s and 1930s.

Self-dealing transactions were apparently common in the
earlier days of operation of the investment companies. These
transactions took various forms. In some instances, an
investment company's assets provided a ready supply of funds
that could be borrowed at low rates by the fund's founders.
The investment company also served as a dumping ground for
the founder's less promising securities, which the founder sold

---

[25] "The Mutual Fund Industry: A Legal Survey," op. cit., 777.

to the investment company at fictitious prices.[26] Another form of self-serving dealing involves the use of a technique called switching to generate brokerage commissions. Switching basically refers to enticement of investors to redeem shares in one management company and to invest in another company, thereby generating sales commissions in return for valueless transactions.[27]

The shareholders of many investment companies were the victims of direct embezzlement in addition to the more subtle forms of misappropriation of shareholders' investments. For example, in one case, a group of investors assumed control of Continental Securities Corporation for $580,000, elected a new board of directors, and looted the company of $3.25 million dollars in securities.[28]

Another type of abuse investment company advisers were alleged to have engaged in was dilution. Dilution was a sales tactic designed to take advantage of the slow dissemination of information prevalent in the 1920s and 1930s. Every night after the stock market closed, an investment company would recompute its net asset value; however, the new net asset value would not be posted until ten o'clock the next morning. In the interim there were, effectively, two prices. Orders for shares could be placed at the lower of the two prices, which had the effect of diluting the value of shares held by current shareholders. The new shareholder would gain an instant profit, i.e., the difference between the two net asset values, at the expense of shareholders already in the fund. To understand how the dilution occurred, consider the following example. Suppose that at the end of Day 1, the net asset value of a fund is $100, and that there are ten shares, so that the net asset value per share is $10. Suppose that by the end of Day 2, the net asset value of the fund had increased by 10 percent

---

[26] Ibid., 789.

[27] Ibid., 790.

[28] Ibid., 789.

to $110 with a corresponding increase in the per share value to
$11. Now suppose a salesperson permits an order for five new
shares to take place at the old price of $10 per share. With the
addition of $50 (5 x $10) in assets, the net asset value of the
fund increases to $160. However, shareholders, rather than
realize an increase of 10 percent given by an increase in price
to $11 per share, only realize an increase of 6.6 percent, given
by an increase in price to $10.67 per share, because of the
dilution effect. This was a strong selling feature that salesmen
touted in order to produce more brokerage commissions. While
the losses caused by dilution on any single transaction were
usually small, collectively they became significant.[29]

The types of behavior documented by the SEC prior to
the 1940 Act strongly suggest that the investment company
industry was not competitive. In competitive markets, market
forces prevent such abuses from occurring, and yields to
investors must match competitive market yields. The 1940 Act,
described below, was created to deal with these abuses.
Subsequent chapters examine the development of the industry,
paying particular attention to the emergence of competitive
constraints that prevent the type of abusive behavior just
described from occurring.

Mechanisms Established to Deal with the Abuses

The 1940 Act went beyond the Securities Act of 1933
(the 1933 Act) and the Securities Exchange Act of 1934 (the
1934 Act) to provide a more comprehensive system of
regulation for investment companies. In addition to reaffirming
the registration and filing requirements of previous legislation,
the 1940 Act establishes a corporate-like oversight structure to
minimize the opportunities for abuses in the investment
company industry.

The 1940 Act contains extensive disclosure requirements.
In addition to a series of registration requirements, every

---

[29] Ibid., 790-792.

investment company must distribute at least semiannually a detailed report of the company's activities to its shareholders. These reports must contain information on the financial status of the fund, the securities held in the fund's portfolio, compensation paid to the directors, and purchases and sales of investment securities within the portfolio.[30] Other disclosure rules require that sales literature distributed in connection with the sale of investment company shares be filed with the SEC.

The 1940 Act contains a number of requirements that establish procedures for independent review of management acts. First, it requires that all shares distributed by an investment company have voting rights and that certain management actions be approved by a majority of outstanding shareholders. Second, it dictates that certain management tasks be carried out by a board of directors, at least 40 percent of whose members are independent.

Under the 1940 Act, there must be a written contract between a mutual fund and its investment adviser, approved by a majority of the fund's outstanding shares. The contract must conform to the following: (1) it must precisely describe all compensation to be paid by the fund; (2) it must continue for longer than two years only if approved at least annually by the board of directors or a majority of the outstanding shares; (3) it must be terminable at any time by the board of directors or shareholders without penalty and without more than 60 days notice; and (4) it must be terminable automatically in the event of its assignment.[31]

The voting rights of shareholders, as set out in the 1940 Act, require every newly issued share of investment stock to be voting stock having equal voting rights with every other outstanding voting stock. In addition to ratification of the advisory contract, shareholders' voting rights extend to the following: [32]

---

[30] *ICA of 1940*, sec. 80a-29(d).

[31] *ICA of 1940*, sec. 80a-15(a).

[32] *ICA of 1940*, sec. 80a-12,-13,-16, and -31.

1. Election of directors
2. Authorization of changes in investment objectives or nature of business
3. Selection of independent accountants
4. Approval of any plan of distribution and related financing

Finally, the 1940 Act gives the SEC power to intervene on behalf of a fund's shareholders. Specifically, while the 1940 Act does not expressly limit the size of management fees, Section 36 authorizes the SEC to sue for injunctive relief in cases involving "gross misconduct or abuse of trust" on the part of the investment adviser.[33]

THE 1970 AMENDMENTS

The rapid growth of mutual funds, which were only in their infancy at the time the 1940 Act was passed, led Congress to re-evaluate regulation of the investment company industry. In the 1960s, Congress called for a detailed study of the mutual fund industry. The findings were reported in the following three studies: (1) a 1962 study entitled *A Study of Mutual Funds: Prepared for the Securities and Exchange Commission by the Wharton School of Finance and Commerce* (Wharton Report), (2) a 1963 SEC special study of securities markets, and (3) a 1966 SEC report entitled *Public Policy Implications of Investment Company Growth* (SEC Policy Report). The SEC Policy Report incorporated the findings of the Wharton Report. However, the SEC Policy Report differed from the Wharton Report in that it made specific recommendations for amending the 1940 Act. The findings of these reports prompted Congress to draft the 1970 Amendments to the 1940 Act.

---

[33] *ICA of 1940*, sec. 80a-36.

Concerns Raised by the 1960s' Reports

Potential conflicts of interest between fund management and shareholders, and the possible absence of arm's-length bargaining between these two agents, were major concerns raised in the three reports. The SEC decided that the unique structure of the relationship between a mutual fund and its affiliated adviser impedes arm's-length bargaining in the establishment of advisory fee contracts. The SEC Policy Report claimed that the provisions of the 1940 Act dealt inadequately with these problems, particularly in light of what it viewed to be a lack of competition among mutual funds.[34] The Wharton Report also suggested that the mutual fund's lack of bargaining power with its adviser and the lack of alternate investment vehicles resulted in high management costs to the investor. Since investors are dependent on the investment adviser to provide most of the management services, the Senate Committee believed that a mutual fund could not easily terminate its relationship with its adviser.[35]

Another major issue addressed in the studies of the mutual fund industry was the independent oversight of advisers. The Wharton Report contended that the provisions for shareholder voting and unaffiliated directors called for by the 1940 Act were ineffective. While more investors were investing in mutual funds, the Wharton Report concluded that investors were apathetic about their voting rights. Attendance at annual meetings was very low, and most voting was carried out by proxy. The Report states the voting was likely controlled by management through the "corporate proxy machinery."[36]

---

[34] SEC, "Policy Report," 12.

[35] *Senate Report*, 4901.

[36] Wharton School of Finance and Commerce, "A Study of Mutual Funds," *House Report* No. 2274, 87th Congress, 2d Session (Washington, DC: U.S. Government Printing Office, 1962), 8. [*Wharton Report*]

The original 1940 Act required that 40 percent of a fund's board of directors be unaffiliated with the fund's adviser and that a majority of the directors be unaffiliated with the fund's principal underwriter. The Wharton Report, however, asserted that the unaffiliated directors had little incentive to challenge an adviser's decisions. Moreover, since the unaffiliated directors of an investment company are usually selected by persons affiliated with the investment adviser and are not involved in active management of the fund, the Wharton Report also questioned whether unaffiliated directors could adequately safeguard shareholders interests in negotiations with the adviser.[37]

The Senate Committee also observed that the provisions contained in the 1940 Act failed to provide a mechanism for challenging the fairness of management contracts in court. In a similar vein, the SEC Policy Report claimed that litigation had been ineffective as a check against abuses by fund advisers because the courts had utilized the very narrow standard of "corporate waste" or a flagrant misuse of resources in judging excessiveness of fees.[38] The Senate Committee agreed that this standard was too narrow and only appropriate in situations where there was arm's-length bargaining. Since in the opinion of the Senate Committee the mutual fund industry was not competitive, the Committee recommended that a broader standard be applied and proposed that a fiduciary duty should be imposed on the investment adviser with respect to the handling of the fund's assets and investments.

The SEC, however, recommended that a stronger standard, i.e., one of "reasonableness," be imposed on investment advisers with respect to adviser-fee contracts. The SEC stated that "the standard of reasonableness would make clear that persons who derive benefits from their fiduciary relationships with investment companies can charge them no more for their services than if they were dealing with them on

---

[37] Ibid., 8.

[38] SEC, "Policy Report," 12.

an arm's length basis."[39]   However, the SEC explicitly noted that this standard should not preclude advisers from making a profit.

Another concern expressed in the reports was the absence of noticeable fee reductions intended to pass on to investors some portion of the economies of scale that were presumed to manifest themselves as assets in a fund grew. To investigate this issue the Wharton Report presented an analysis of advisory fees. The Wharton Report observed that fees set by advisory contracts were grouped tightly about the traditional 0.5 percent of average net assets, and the level of fees was not correlated with the size of a fund.[40] Yet, the report claimed that operating expenses appeared to decline as a fund grew.[41] This analysis also compared the advisory fees charged to mutual funds versus other clients, and found that rates charged to mutual funds were substantially higher. However, such fee comparisons are clouded by the fact that the same bundle of services is not being offered. For example, one important difference is the ability of mutual fund shareholders to engage in virtually unlimited transactions. While this would lead to higher costs, the fee comparisons made no adjustments for this important factor.

The SEC Policy Report concluded that investors were not enjoying the benefits associated with the alleged scale economies.[42] Although the Senate Committee felt that in some instances investors were not receiving the benefits of economies of scale, it did acknowledge that some fund managers were indexing their fees to a fund's asset size and that this practice should provide a guide.[43]   Not one of the three studies

---

[39] Ibid., 13.

[40] *Wharton Report*, 28-29.

[41] Ibid., 29.

[42] SEC, "Policy Report," 11.

[43] *Senate Report*, 4902.

attempted a formal analysis of economies of scale. Instead, the presumption of the presence of economies of scale continued to be based on intuition rather than empirical evidence.

The sources and effects of fund growth and portfolio activity were also investigated. The Wharton Report determined that mutual fund assets were highly concentrated, with the top five advisers managing 43 percent of total assets invested in mutual funds on December 31, 1960.[44] Furthermore, it was observed that turnover of mutual fund shares was lower than the typical rates for stocks listed on the New York Stock Exchange between the years 1952 and 1958.[45] In addition, the SEC noted that the high level of sales loads and possible capital gains tax liability prevented shareholders from disciplining investment companies that overpriced advisory services by switching funds when charges were excessive.

The reports also inquired as to whether competition in sales loads was hampered by the regulations. The Senate Committee noted that the normal sales load for a mutual fund was 8.5 percent. This was protected by a provision of the 1940 Act that prohibits dealers from cutting the sales load fixed by the mutual fund underwriter.[46] The Senate Committee concluded that this particular rule might actually lead to competition among distribution agents for the opportunity to distribute a fund's shares rather than leading to competition for investor's assets. In this respect, the Senate Committee claimed that the regulations did not protect shareholders, but worked to the advantage of dealers and salesmen.[47]

---

[44] *Wharton Report*, 27.

[45] Ibid., 15.

[46] *Senate Report*, 4904.

[47] Ibid., 4904.

New Regulations in the 1970 Amendments

In response to the three reports, the Senate Committee identified three primary objectives of the 1970 Amendments:

1. To modify the rules of the 1940 Act related to investment company management fees, mutual fund sales commissions, and periodic payment or contractual plan sales commissions
2. To permit banks and savings and loan associations to operate commingled managing agency accounts in competition with mutual funds
3. To facilitate, update, and improve the administration and enforcement of the ICA of 1940 [48]

The 1970 Amendments modified the rules related to the board of directors in an attempt to improve the board's oversight ability. The requirement calling for unaffiliated directors was changed to impose the presence of "disinterested" directors. This change was an attempt to ensure that oversight was truly independent of the investment adviser. Furthermore, Section 15 of the 1940 Act was amended to establish explicit prerequisites for approval of the management fee contract.[49]

Section 36(b) added under the 1970 Amendments is a codification of the explicit fiduciary duty imposed on investment advisers. This section holds that

> The investment adviser of a registered investment company shall be deemed to have a fiduciary duty with respect to the receipt of compensation for services, or of payment of a material nature, paid by such registered investment company, or by the security holders thereof, to such investment adviser or any affiliated person of such investment adviser.[50]

---

[48] Ibid., 4898.

[49] *ICA of 1940*, sec. 80a-15(c).

[50] Ibid., sec. 80a-35(b) (15 U.S.C., sec. 80a-35(b)).

Both the SEC and the shareholders are given a right to act against an investment adviser. However, the plaintiff carries the burden of proof establishing the breach of fiduciary duty. The Senate Committee stated that Section 36(b) is not intended to substitute the court's business judgment for that of the board of directors in the area of management fees. While the ultimate decision whether there has or has not been a breach of fiduciary duty rests on the courts, the approval by the board of directors, including a majority of the disinterested directors, and shareholder ratification are to be given appropriate weight. While fees may be challenged in court as excessive, the Senate Committee recognized that an investment adviser is entitled to earn a profit. The Committee asserted that regulation under the 1970 Amendments was not intended to impose a "cost-plus" structure upon management contracts; nor were the amendments intended to introduce rate regulation of the sort applied to public utilities. Rather, the sole purpose of the section was to spell out explicitly the fiduciary duty of the investment adviser and provide a mechanism for a challenge of an advisory fee contract.[51]

The 1970 Amendments did not adopt as strong an approach with respect to regulation of sales loads. Previous regulation only provided protection against unconscionable or grossly excessive sales loads. The Committee, however, decided that the existing self-regulatory mechanism, with SEC oversight, was sufficient to protect the investor against unreasonable sales loads.[52]

RECENT REGULATORY INITIATIVES

Since 1970, the SEC has offered several proposals to modify the Investment Company Act of 1940. The most extensive changes proposed in the regulation of the mutual

---

[51] *Senate Report*, 4902-4903.

[52] Ibid., 4904.

fund industry since the 1940 Act were contained in a concept paper submitted by the SEC in 1982.[53] The SEC concluded that a re-evaluation of regulation in the mutual fund industry was appropriate. Although the SEC observed that shareholders and directors have had little influence over the management of mutual funds since the 1970 Amendments, the concept paper did not call for changes in SEC rules or for new legislation designed to increase the power of investors.

The concept paper proposed two alternative regulatory schemes. The first called for the adoption of rules exempting mutual funds from the Act's shareholder voting requirements. The second proposed a new type of investment company called the unitary investment fund (UIF). A UIF would have neither voting shareholders nor a board of directors. Accordingly, oversight duties formerly held by the board of directors would shift to the SEC. Therefore, under this proposed form of organization, a UIF would have no fiduciary duty with regard to management fees.

In its comments on its own proposals, the SEC asserted that the industry was not sufficiently competitive and that investors' decisions were not sufficiently sensitive to expenses. In particular, the SEC argued, since investors' decisions focus upon a fund's objective and performance, expenses are considered by them only indirectly. As a result, one could not justify any strong deregulatory steps. The SEC concluded that if the UIF arrangement were permitted, Section 36, the fiduciary obligation section, should still be maintained.

The major concerns expressed in the concept paper about a UIF structure included

1. Adequacy of notice of management actions to shareholders
2. The strength of deterrents available to keep investment managers from acting in conflict with shareholders' interests

---

[53] "Investment Company Act Release No. 12888, December 10, 1982," *Federal Securities Law Reports*, vol. 999 (December 21, 1988) 85,613-85,640.

3. Adequacy of the recourses from management's acts available to shareholders[54]

The second concern arose from the proposal that UIFs be exempt from the fiduciary obligation imposed in Section 36. Nonetheless, the paper offered a number of reasons for elimination of Section 36. First, the concept paper argued that Section 36 was anomalous to begin with, imposing an unrealistic fiduciary duty upon investment managers. Second, it noted that Section 36 imposed costs upon the shareholder without producing commensurate benefits. It argued that in the absence of Section 36, competition in the market place would force investment managers to maintain reasonable management fee schedules.[55] Finally, it suggested that a fiduciary duty is appropriate only where the person upon whom the duty rests purports to be acting in the interest of others.

The concept paper noted that the industry had changed in important respects. A significant source of change was the shift toward no-load funds. Another pertinent change was the concentration of industry assets in MMFs, which maintain a constant net asset value. This feature of money market funds removes any detrimental tax ramifications associated with redemption of shares. As a result, the exit barriers that limit shareholders' ability to express dissatisfaction with management performance through redemption of their holdings are removed.

In assessing the proposed changes, the SEC recognized that the process of obtaining shareholder approval is costly. Moreover, because of shareholder apathy, it is unclear whether these costs are outweighed by the assumed benefits of independent oversight by shareholders. On the other hand, the SEC suggested that even if shareholders do not actively exercise their voting rights, the availability of these rights may deter management from acting in a manner contrary to the interests of shareholders.

---

[54] Ibid., 85,631.

[55] Ibid., 85,636.

The SEC did note, however, that concerns raised by the proposed elimination of shareholder voting would be alleviated if shareholders were given sufficient notice of management actions. Under such an arrangement, at least two forms of recourse would be available to shareholders. First, they could redeem their shares. Second, if redemption were undesirable, then shareholders could mobilize a challenge to management's actions. The prospect for effectiveness of these avenues was questioned, mainly because of the continuation of sales loads for a significant number of non-MMFs as well as the tax implications of redemptions.[56]

Despite the many arguments favoring elimination of shareholder voting and of boards of directors for funds, the SEC concept paper did not lead to any changes in the regulation of mutual funds. Moreover, proposed regulatory changes (related to 12b-1 plans)[57] suggest a tightening, rather than a loosening, of regulation affecting mutual funds.

The SEC also adopted new rules and amendments to the 1940 Act in May 1988. The purpose of the new rules and

---

[56] Ibid., 85,628.

[57] In 1980, the SEC adopted Rule 12b-1, which allows mutual funds to adopt a plan for the financing of the distribution of shares using a portion of a fund's assets. Reimbursement plans permit investors to defer payment for distribution costs, possibly for several years. Under a 12b-1 reimbursement plan, the fund contracts with a third party, usually the fund's underwriter, to provide distribution services. The fund then reimburses the third party for the distribution expenses incurred in a predetermined manner.

In June 1988, the SEC proposed material amendments to Rule 12b-1 in response to abuses alleged to have occurred since the adoption of 12b-1 plans. The major issues addressed by the proposed changes are limitation of the time period for reimbursement plans, delineation of directors' responsibilities, prohibition of the use of no-load terminology for funds with 12b-1 plans, the requirement of annual shareholder approval for 12b-1 plans, and the elimination of existing carry-over balances. In particular, the SEC was concerned that current practices related to reimbursement arrangements threatened to undermine the role of disinterested directors. See Securities and Exchange Commission, "Payment of Asset-Based Sales Loads by Registered Open-End Management Investment Companies," 17 CFR Part 239, 270, 274, release no. IC-16431, file no. 57-10-88 (June 13, 1988), 1-5.

amendments was to standardize mutual fund performance calculations so that investors could more easily compare mutual fund performance claims. The new rules originated from concern over the explosive growth of non-money market funds and the associated advertising expenditures. The SEC feared that managers could take advantage of investors through misleading claims about fund performance.

IS REGULATION NECESSARY IN THE CURRENT ENVIRONMENT?

In evaluating the role of regulation in the mutual fund industry, it is critical to understand the changes that the industry has undergone. The above discussion suggests that at least some critics thought that fund advisers were indeed engaged in self-seeking behavior at the expense of shareholders and that serious misappropriation of wealth occurred in the 1920s and 1930s before the enactment of the 1940 Act. This is not to say that the likelihood of such abuses remains high today. Whatever conditions were present in these earlier years, it is unlikely that any abuse would survive today. For example, individual investors in the early investment companies had little power or incentive to monitor an adviser's behavior. Small individual investors have only a small payoff from monitoring in relation to the costs of monitoring, and therefore as individuals they are unlikely to undertake monitoring activities. However, the increased number of investors with sizable asset holdings has given rise to a group of shareholders with the incentive to monitor adviser behavior.

Aside from alterations in the composition of a fund's shareholders, a number of other developments served to discipline an adviser's conduct and reduce expropriation hazards. One of these is the growth in liquidity of the underlying fund shares. If the shares of a fund cannot easily be liquidated, it becomes very costly if not impossible for investors to switch to another fund as shareholders detect abuses by the adviser. Some of the determinants of the liquidity of a shareholder's investment are whether a fund is closed-end or open-end, the presence of redemption fees that effectively punish shareholders for liquidating their investment, and the market shares of load and no-load funds. The degree of competition among mutual funds and mutual fund advisers for shareholders, competition from financial institutions of other types, and shareholder demand elasticity are other critical elements for an assessment of the likelihood of continued abuse by mutual fund advisers.

In its consideration of recent proposals to modify the regulation of mutual funds, the SEC has to some extent re-evaluated market conditions in the mutual fund industry. However, its unwillingness to act upon some of the earlier initiatives related to the corporate governance structure of mutual funds and, more recently, the tightening of 12b-1 plans indicate that the SEC does not consider the changes that have occurred in the industry sufficient to change the way the mutual fund industry is regulated. The analyses in subsequent chapters challenge this assessment through more formal investigation of the industrial economics of the mutual fund industry.

THREE

LITIGATION UNDER THE 1940 ACT AND THE 1970 AMENDMENTS

While most of the litigation generated under the 1940 Act and the 1970 Amendments terminated in settlements, the courts have delivered a number of opinions that indicate the judiciary's views on regulation and patterns of behavior in the mutual fund industry. The litigation has been based on allegations that advisers charged excessive management fees. The standards used to adjudge fees before the 1970 Amendments were very narrow, and the plaintiffs were never successful in cases that were fully litigated. It was partly for this reason that Congress passed the 1970 Amendments. However, plaintiffs continued to be largely unsuccessful under the relaxed standards of the modified Section 36(b). Let us turn to a history of this litigation.

PRE-1970 AMENDMENTS

Before the 1970 Amendments, a number of suits were brought against fund advisers claiming that the fees were excessive. Table 3.1 lists the suits initiated during the 1960s. Only three cases were actually tried on the facts, or merits, of the case. These cases were brought under either common law or the original Section 36, which permitted suit for "gross misconduct or gross abuse of trust." While the original section

Table 3.1

Mutual Funds Involved in Excessive Fee Litigation Prior to the 1970 Amendments

Case Name	Citation	Status	Fund Name
Meiselman v. Eberstadt	39 Del. Ch. 563, 170 A.2d 720 (1961)	Decided for defendant	Chemical Fund
Saxe v. Brady	40 Del. Ch. 474, 184 A.2d 602 (1962)	Decided for defendant	Fundamental Investors
Glicken v. Bradford	35 F.R.D. 144 (1962)	Settled	
Kerner v. Crossman	211 F.Supp. 397 (1962)	Settled	Axe-Houghton Fund B
Saxe v. Crossman	F.S.L.R. (CCH) 91,159 (1962)	Settled	
Acampora v. Birkland	220 F.Supp. 527 (1963)	Decided for defendant	Financial Industrial Fund
Saminsky v. Abbott	194 A.2d 549 (1963)	Settled	
Phillips v. Bradford	228 F.Supp. 397 (1964)	Settled	
Rome v. Archer	41 Del. Ch. 404, 197 A.2d 49 (1964)	Settled	Wellington Fund
Elster v. Dreyfus	F.S.L.R. (CCH) 91,914 (1967)	Settled	
Lessan v. Television-Electronics Fund	F.S.L.R. (CCH) 92,305 (1968)	Settled	
Goodman v. Van Der Heyde	F.S.L.R. (CCH) 92,541 (1969)	Settled	
Josephson v. Campbell	F.S.L.R. (CCH) 92,347 (1969)	Settled	
Kurach v. Weissman	49 F.R.D. 304 (1970)	Settled	

Sources: Fidelity Management and Research; James N. Benedict and Mark Holland, "Standards of Fiduciary Duty Under Section 36(b) of the Investment Company Act," New Dimensions in Securities Litigation: Planning and Strategies (1987); and Tamar Frankel, "Money Market Funds", The Review of Securities Regulation, vol. 14, no. 10 (May 20, 1981), 921-924.

only empowered the SEC to bring suit, shareholders were successful in arguing an implied private right of action. In all of the cases tried, however, the court found for the defendant, the mutual fund adviser.

In the first case, *Meiselman v. Eberstadt,*[58] it was determined that fees higher than the industry average did not necessarily constitute a violation of the 1940 Act and that other facets of the adviser's services must be considered. In this case, the plaintiff alleged that a fund adviser had been paid an excessive fee in breach of common law fiduciary duty. The central argument of the complaint was that the adviser should be paid only for the time spent on the fund's affairs and only at a rate comparable to other executives with similar responsibilities. While the court conceded that there might be some upper level beyond which an adviser's compensation was excessive, it did not agree that a level above the industry average should necessarily be deemed excessive. The court dismissed the complaint, holding that the quality of the service provided and not the quantity should determine compensation levels. Since a majority of the unaffiliated directors and shareholders had approved the advisory contract, the adviser had not breached its fiduciary duty.

The next case, *Saxe v. Brady,*[59] set the standard for the review of fees. The plaintiff brought suit against the directors, advisers, and the principal underwriter of the fund for allegedly unreasonable, excessive, and wasteful fees. The advisory contract set fees at a flat rate equal to 0.5 percent of average net assets. The plaintiff considered a flat fee inappropriate because of alleged economies of scale with respect to the fund's assets under management. Thus, the plaintiff argued that, in light of the rapid increase in the fund's assets, the traditional 0.5 percent fixed level constituted "an illegal waste" of corporate assets.

---

[58] *Meiselman v. Eberstadt,* 39 Del. Ch. 563, 170 A.2d 720 (1961).

[59] *Saxe v. Brady,* 40 Del. Ch. 474, 184 A.2d 602 (1962).

However, the court held that since the shareholders had been fully informed of all material facts, the burden of proof for establishing that fees were excessive fell upon the plaintiff and that the appropriate standard by which fees should be judged was "corporate waste" and not fairness. The court proposed three elements to be considered when evaluating fees: (1) the profits earned by the adviser compared with profits earned by similar management companies; (2) the ratio of expenses to profits of the adviser compared to that of similar management companies; and (3) the services provided by the adviser. With respect to the third of these elements, the court's view was that services, while important, are not necessarily determinative of the reasonableness of the fees. The court dismissed the complaint, but warned that the fees were nearing an excessive point and should be adjusted to reflect economies of scale.

The last opinion delivered before the 1970 Amendments, *Acampora v. Birkland*,[60] was the only Federal Court decision to address advisory fees under the 1940 Act. The plaintiff contended that since the fund's adviser offered fewer services than the industry average, the traditional fee of 0.5 percent was "equitably excessive." The court adopted the *Saxe* rationale without criticism in determining an opinion. Dismissing the complaint, the court held that while the fees might be high, they were not "unconscionable" or "shocking."

Even though plaintiffs were not successful in these fully litigated cases, advisers did make some concessions in the cases that were settled. The settlements frequently called for replacement of the flat 0.5 percent fee by sliding-scale schedules. Moreover, some settlements provided "that net profits derived by fund underwriters be offset against management fees; that the adviser guarantee credits against the fees; that the adviser apply the proceeds of any 'give-ups' received in connection with its brokerage activities toward

---

[60] 220 F. Supp. 527 (D. Colo. 1963), *Acampora v. Birkland*.

reduction of the management fees; or that the Board of Directors be reconstituted." [61]

POST-1970 AMENDMENTS

After the 1970 Amendments were enacted, a number of cases, listed in Table 3.2, arose under the new Section 36(b). Over 50 suits have been instituted, involving almost 30 different funds. A majority of these funds have been money market funds, which is not surprising since these funds experienced rapid growth in the late 1970s and early 1980s and constitute the largest funds in the industry.

A material development in the approach of the courts in the cases that arose after the 1970 Amendments was their emphasis on disclosure in analyzing an adviser's fiduciary duty.[62] These cases turned on whether the adviser had adequately informed the independent directors of all material information. If the directors had not been adequately informed, then the court held that there was a breach of fiduciary duty under Section 36(b).

Very few cases alleging excessive fees under the new Section 36(b) have been tried on their merits. The first of these cases, *Wolfson v. Cooper*,[63] cited both *Acampora* and *Saxe*,

---

[61] James N. Benedict and Mark Holland, "Standards of Fiduciary Duty Under Section 36(b) of the Investment Company Act," *New Dimensions in Securities Litigation: Planning and Strategies*, ALI-ABA Course of Study (1987), 6. [Benedict and Holland]

[62] See *Fogel v. Chestnutt*, 533 F.2d 731 (2d Cir. 1975), cert. denied, 429 U.S. 824 (1976); *Galfand v. Chestnutt Corp.*, 545 F.2d 807 (2d Cir. 1976), cert. denied, 435 U.S. 943 (1978); *Papilsky v. Berndt*, [1976-1977 Transfer Binder] Fed. Sec. L. Rep. (CCH) Para. 95,627 (S.D.N.Y. June 24, 1976); *Tannenbaum v. Zeller*, 552 F.2d 402 (2d Cir.), cert. denied, 434 U.S. 934 (1977); *Fogel v. Chestnutt*, 668 F.2d 100 (2d Cir. 1981), cert. denied, 459 U.S. 828 (1982).

[63] [1976-1977] Fed. Sec. L. Rep. (CCH) Para. 95,634 (S.D.N.Y. June 22, 1976), aff'd without opinion sub nom. *Wolfson v. Stein, Roe & Farnham*, no. 76-7382 (2d Cir. 1977).

Table 3.2

Mutual Funds Involved in Excessive Fee Litigation After the 1970 Amendments

Plaintiff	Defendant	Year Initiated	Status	Fund Name
Boyko	Reserve Fund, Inc.	1975*		Reserve Fund
Fogel	Chestnutt Corp.	1975*	Decided for plaintiff	American Investors Fund
Galfand	Chestnutt Corp.	1976*	Decided for plaintiff	American Investors Fund
Gross	Dreyfus Corp.	1976		Liquid Assets Fund
Krasner	Dreyfus Corp.	1976	Settled	Liquid Assets Fund
Papilsky	Berndt	1976*	Decided for plaintiff	
Untermeyer	Fidelity Daily Income Trust	1976	Settled	Fidelity Daily Income Tr.
Untermeyer	Dreyfus Corp.	1976		Liquid Assets Fund
Wolfson	Cooper	1976*	Decided for defendant	
Grossman	Johnson	1977	Dismissed	
Halligan	Standard & Poor's/Intercapital, Inc.	1977*	Settled	S&P Intercapital Inc. Sec.
Tannenbaum	Zeller	1977*	Decided for defendant	Chemical Fund
Untermeyer	Dreyfus Liquid Assets	1978		Liquid Assets Fund
Blatt	Dean Witter Reynolds Intercapital	1979	Settled	InterCapital Liquid Assets
Gartenberg	Merrill Lynch Asset Mgmt, Inc.	1979	Decided for defendant	ML Ready Asset Trust
Cohen	Fund Asset Management, Inc.	1980*		
Emanuel Brown Employees	Fidelity Mgmt. & Research Co.	1980	Settled	Fidelity Daily Income Tr.
Finkel	O'Connor	1980	Settled	
Haber	Fidelity Management & Research Co.	1980	Settled	Fidelity Daily Income Tr.
Kreindler	Fidelity Management & Research Co.	1980	Settled	Fidelity Daily Income Tr.

continued on next page

Table 3.2 continued

Plaintiff	Defendant	Year Initiated	Status	Fund Name
Lerner	Reserve Management Co.	1980	Dismissed	Reserve Fund
Levy	Berstein-Macaulay, Inc.	1980	Settled	Shearson Daily Dividends
Lewis	Oppenheimer Management Corp.	1980	Settled	Op. Money Mkt Fund
Markovitz	Moneymart Assets Inc.	1980	Settled	Moneymart Assets
Markovitz	Markovitz v. Brody	1980	Settled	Shearson Daily Dividends
Meyer	Oppenheimer Management Corp.	1980	Settled	Daily Cash Accumulation
Rosenfeld	Merrill Lynch Asset Management, Inc.	1980	Dismissed	ML CMA Money Trust
Schuyt	Rowe Price Prime Reserve Fund	1980	Decided for defendant	Prime Reserve Fund
Tarlov	Paine Webber Cashfund, Inc.	1980		PW Cashfund
Weiss	Temporary Investment Fund	1980		Temporary Investment Fund
Ashare	Brill	1981	Dismissed	Dreyfus Liquid Assets
Evangelist	Fidelity Management & Research Co.	1981	Settled	Fidelity Cash Reserves
Fogel	Chestnutt Corp.	1981*	Decided for plaintiff	American Investors Fund
Greenfield	Delaware Cash Reserves	1981	Settled	Delaware Cash Reserves
Gross	National Liquid Reserves	1981	Settled	National Liquid Reserves
Jerzol	Cash Reserve Management	1981	Settled	EF Hutton Cash Reserve Mgmt
Kalman	Merrill Lynch Asset Management, Inc.	1981	Settled	ML CMA Money Trust
Kalman	CMA Money Trust	1981	Dismissed	ML CMA Money Trust
Kamen	Scudder, Stevens & Clark	1981	Settled	Scudder Cash Invest. Trust
Naeder	Institutional Research Corp.	1981	Settled	AARP US Gov't Money Market
Naeder	NRTA-AARP U.S. Gov't MMT	1981	Settled	AARP US Gov't Money Market
Rampell	Webster Management Corp.	1981	Settled	Webster Cash Reserve

continued on next page

Table 3.2 continued

Plaintiff	Defendant	Year Initiated	Status	Fund Name
Schuyt	NRTA-AARP U.S. Gov't MMT	1981	Settled	AARP US Gov't Money Market
Shaev	NRTA-AARP U.S. Gov't MMT	1981	Settled	AARP US Gov't Money Market
Veleba	Mutual Management Corp.	1981	Settled	
Friedman	E.F. Hutton	1982	Settled	
Gartenberg	Merrill Lynch Asset Management, Inc.	1982	Decided for defendant	ML Ready Asset Trust
Glassman	Paine Webber Cashfund, Inc.	1982		PW Cashfund
Meyer	Oppenheimer	1982		Daily Cash Accumulation
Bromson	Lehman Management Co.	1984	Settled	Lehman Cash Mgm't Fund
Daily Income Fund Inc.	Fox	1984*	Settled	Daily Income Fund
Labaton	Fidelity Management & Research Co.	1984	Settled	Magellen Fund
Kamen	Kemper Financial Services, Inc.	1985		Cash Equivalent Fund
Krinsk	Fund Asset Management, Inc.	1985	Decided for defendant	ML CMA Money Trust
Weissman	Alliance Capital Management Corp.	1986*	Settled	Alliance Capital Reserves

Note: * Year of decision.
Sources: Fidelity Management and Research; James N. Benedict and Mark Holland, "Standards of Fiduciary Duty Under Section
         36(b) of the Investment Company Act," New Dimensions in Securities Litigation: Planning and Strategies (1987); and
         Tamar Frankel, "Money Market Funds", The Review of Securities Regulation, vol. 14, no. 10 (May 20, 1981), 921-924.

which were decided before the 1970 Amendments, as authority. The defendant was adviser to two separate equity funds having sliding-scale fee schedules. The plaintiff contended that it was the defendant's fiduciary duty to merge the assets of the two funds in order that shareholders be able to realize the lower fee ratio that would result from the sliding-scale schedule. The complaint was dismissed because the Directors had been fully informed of the material facts and had unanimously approved the advisory contracts. The court apparently viewed the amendment of Section 36(b) as not substantially altering the duties of investment advisers.[64]

The first interpretation of the amended Section 36(b) resulted from two suits that produced opinions from both the District Court and the Court of Appeals in a matter involving Merrill Lynch Ready Assets Trust (the Ready Asset Fund), an MMF, and Merrill Lynch Asset Management, Inc. In the first case, *Gartenberg v. Merrill Lynch Asset Management, Inc.* (*Gartenberg I*),[65] shareholders of the Ready Asset Fund brought actions against the fund, the fund's adviser, and the adviser's broker affiliate, alleging that the compensation received by the adviser for 1980-1981 constituted a breach of fiduciary duty. The District Court ultimately dismissed the complaint on the ground that the complaining shareholders had failed to sustain their burden of proof, which was affirmed on appeal.

In the District Court the plaintiffs alleged that in light of the size of the Ready Asset Fund, the adviser made too much money in relation to his costs under the agreed-upon fee schedule, presumably as a result of economies of scale. After reviewing the legislative history of the 1970 Amendments, the District Court determined that the common law tradition of "fiduciary duty" was the appropriate standard by which to judge advisory fees. The court continued to explain that "the essence

---

[64] Benedict and Holland, 19.

[65] 528 Federal Supplement 1038 (1981), *Gartenberg v. Merrill Lynch Asset Management, Inc., et al.*, U.S. District Court, S.D. New York. Nos. 79 Civ. 3123(MP), 79 Civ. 5726(MP) (December 28, 1981). [*Gartenberg 1981*]

of the [fiduciary] test is whether or not under all the circumstances the transaction carries the earmarks of an arm's length bargain."[66]   In applying this test to the facts of the case, the court considered the following three elements of the advisory contract: (1) the fairness of the advisory fee; (2) the approval of the advisory agreement by the trustees; and (3) the shareholders' consideration of the fee.

The court first examined the fairness of the advisory fee, which included evaluation of the nature, quality, and extent of the services provided in relation to the fee paid. Economies of scale and any benefits to Merrill Lynch as a whole that were attributable to the fund were also considered. In its analysis of the services provided relative to the fee paid, the court examined the magnitude and quality of the services provided, the fee paid to the fund's adviser, the net earnings resulting from provision of these services, the costs of providing processing services, and distribution expenses.

The plaintiffs attributed the magnitude of the adviser's profit to the size of the fund and claimed that the benefits derived from realization of the alleged scale economies were not passed on to the fund's shareholders. With respect to the claim of scale economies, the defendants presented evidence that was claimed to demonstrate that (1) as the assets in the fund grow, the demand for the administrative and processing services supplied by the adviser also grow proportionately; and (2) larger and costlier facilities are needed to deal with the increased volume. Nevertheless, no evidence was provided by the plaintiffs to demonstrate either the presence of scale economies or the fund's failure to share benefits derived from those supposed scale economies. Therefore, the court concluded that the compensation paid by the fund to the adviser bore a fair relation to the costs of providing advisory and management services, and that the fees were consistent with the compensation received by other firms performing

---

[66] Ibid., 1047 (quoting *Pepper v. Litton*, 308 U.S. 295, 306-07, 60 S.Ct. 238, 245-46, 84 L.Ed. 281 (1939)).

similar services.[67]

In reaching its decision, the District Court placed considerable weight on the competitive process and, in particular, on the bargaining power of shareholders, which arose from their ability to move their assets from one fund to another quickly and at little cost. The court stated that

> It seems clear...that Congress had in mind front-end load equity funds and not today's money market funds which are no-load and in which a shareholder can redeem his shares without the payment of any penalty or tax consequences, and freely invest his funds without expense, on virtually the same terms, in any one of the large number of other funds available in the market place.[68]

The District Court also noted that the money market fund industry is highly competitive, since entry is not limited. In addition, there had been ample disclosure by the adviser to prospective customers, shareholders, the fund, and its trustees[69] with respect to the fees charged. The District Court judge wrote in his opinion that under such conditions reliance should be placed on the normal forces of the economic system for control of fees.[70]

Although the Appellate Court upheld the District Court decision, the merits of the case were reviewed under a much more rigorous set of standards.[71] The appellants altogether rejected the notion that competition was present and instead

---

[67] Ibid., 1068.

[68] Ibid., 1044.

[69] Ibid., 1067.

[70] Ibid., 1068.

[71] 694 Federal Reporter, 2nd Series 923 (1982), *Gartenberg v. Merrill Lynch Asset Management, Inc., et al.*, and *Andre v. Merrill Lynch Ready Asset Trust, et al.* U.S. Court of Appeals, Second Circuit. Nos. 11, 14, Dockets 82-7142, 82-7074. Argued September 15, 1982. Decided December 3, 1982. [*Gartenberg 1982*]

argued that

> ...since each investment company fund is a captive of its manager,
> from which it cannot as a practical matter divorce itself, and since
> there is no possibility that a competitor will take the fund's business
> from its manager by offering a lower rate, the manager sets its own
> fee and the fund has no practical alternative but to pay it.[72]

The court held that

> ...to be guilty of a violation of Section 36(b)...the adviser-manager
> must charge a fee that is so disproportionately large that it bears no
> reasonable relationship to the services rendered and could not have
> been the product of arm's length bargaining.[73]

The Court of Appeals disagreed with the District Court
that the price charged by other similar advisers can serve as a
defensible benchmark for evaluation of fees charged by the
adviser of the Ready Asset Fund. The Court of Appeals based
this conclusion on the ground that competition for shareholders
at the fund level does not imply that there is competition
among managers for fund business.[74] In other words, since a
fund cannot move from one adviser to another, the Appellate
Court claimed that less weight should be given to rates charged
by advisers of other similar funds. The Court of Appeals also
dismissed the relevance of competition among the funds, noting
that the adviser's fee is relatively insignificant to each shareholder. Moreover, the court stated that the distinction between
front-end load funds and no-load funds is irrelevant in terms of
competitive effects.[75]

---

[72] Ibid., 927-928.

[73] Ibid., 928.

[74] Ibid., 929.

[75] Front-end funds are those that charge commissions at the time the
shares are purchased. The charge is added to the net asset value per share
in the determination of the offering price. In contrast, no-load funds have

The Court of Appeals' affirmation of the District Court decision was ultimately based on the narrower standard that the plaintiffs failed to prove that there was a breach of fiduciary duty and not, as in the District Court case, a finding that the fees charged by Merrill Lynch Asset Management were fair. In reaching its decision, the Court of Appeals gave weight to the fact that the costs of processing money market fund orders were substantial and that the investment adviser's profits were not so large as to amount to a breach of fiduciary duty.[76] However, the Court of Appeals noted that "fall-out" benefits[77] and "float" [78] are important considerations, and information about their magnitude should be disclosed to the independent directors for their consideration when setting fee levels.

Shortly after the delivery of the Court of Appeals' opinion, the plaintiffs filed a new claim (*Gartenberg II*)[79] against Merrill Lynch Ready Asset Trust and its adviser, attacking the adviser's 1982 compensation. The new claims also alleged that misrepresentations were made to the trustees of the fund with regard to the fall-out benefits to the Merrill Lynch organization and to the processing costs incurred by

---

no up-front sales charge. As discussed in later sections, the significance of the distinction stems from the effect on investor mobility.

[76] *Gartenberg* 1982, 933.

[77] Fall-out benefits refer to any benefits the adviser may derive by virtue of its association with the fund.

[78] Float refers to the interest earned by Merrill Lynch on money that is held for a short period of time during check clearing or rerouting of funds.

[79] 573 Federal Supplement 1293, *Gartenberg v. Merrill Lynch Asset Management, Inc., et al.*, and *Andre v. Merrill Lynch Ready Assets Trust, et al.*, U.S. District Court, S.D. New York. Nos. 82 Civ. 8074(MP), 81 Civ. 7021(MP) (September, 1983). [*Gartenberg 1983*]

Merrill Lynch.[80]   Again the action was dismissed on the grounds that the evidence failed to establish that there was a violation of the 1940 Act. The Appellate Court once again upheld the District Court decision.

Despite the fact that all charges against Merrill Lynch were dismissed, the judgments rendered by the District and Appellate Courts did not clear up the grounds upon which suits involving Section 36(b) violations should be resolved. On the one hand, the District Court relied on competition at the fund level as a primary consideration in evaluating alleged violations of the Act. Yet, the Appellate Court rejected the contention that competition at the fund level has any restraining effect on advisers' fees. The immediate question to be resolved is under what conditions competition at the fund level is sufficient to ensure that fees charged by advisers will not be excessive.

The first case decided after the pair of Gartenberg cases was *Schuyt v. Rowe Price Prime Reserve Fund, Inc. (Schuyt)*.[81] The court dismissed the economic analysis of the District Court in *Gartenberg I* and instead relied on the authority of the Court of Appeals. Economic experts for both sides provided testimony on the nature of competition in the mutual fund industry, which the judge dismissed as irrelevant. Instead, the judge focused on the legal analysis presented by the Court of Appeals in *Gartenberg I*. The court stressed the following four factors in determining that the fee charged by the adviser was not excessive: (1) the nature and quality of the services provided by the adviser; (2) the cost of these services; (3) the transfer of benefits of economies of scale to the fund; and (4) the role of the independent directors.[82]   After reviewing the

---

[80] In the first Gartenberg trial, the Appellate Court noted that fall-out benefits to an affiliate in the organization should be taken into account when evaluating the fairness of the adviser's fee.

[81] 663 Federal Supplement 962, *Schuyt v. Rowe Price Prime Reserve Fund, et al.* U.S. District Court, S.D. New York. No. 80, Civ. 506 (RJW) (July 1, 1987).

[82] Ibid., 974.

evidence relating to these factors, the court concluded that the plaintiffs had not met their burden of proof under Section 36(b).

Of particular interest to the current study of the mutual fund industry is the court's analysis of costs and economies of scale. Its consideration of the other two elements entailed little more than qualitative descriptions of the activities of the adviser and the board of directors. The court recognized that measurement of costs in a multiproduct firm is very difficult and considered two different methods in its assessment. The first is based on fully distributed cost techniques, which allocate a portion of a firm's total costs to the production of each product. The second approach is based on incremental costs. The incremental cost of a particular fund in a mutual fund complex is the difference between the total cost incurred by the complex in producing all outputs, including the fund in question, and the total costs the complex would incur were it to abandon operation of that particular fund. After examining both fully distributed and incremental costs, the court concluded that, while imprecise, fully distributed costs were the best approximation to real costs. The court dismissed incremental costs, stating that in a multiproduct firm, incremental costs of a given product do not consider common costs, which are part of the real costs of supplying that product. Instead, the court used fully distributed costs to estimate profits for the three years in question and on this basis concluded that profit levels were not excessive.

The court in the *Schuyt* matter made no attempt to quantify the magnitude of economies of scale. Rather, the court's conclusions relating to economies of scale with respect to fund assets were based on the observation that there were breakpoints in the advisory fee contract of the fund. The court concluded that since the breakpoints were established on the recommendation of the adviser, economies of scale must be present. The adviser, on the other hand, stated that breakpoints were necessary for the fund to remain competitive as it grew.[83]   The court concluded that since the Board of Directors had continually negotiated new breakpoints as the fund grew and the fee charged was among the lowest of all MMFs, the adviser must already be passing on the benefits of the purported economies of scale of the fund.

The courts revisited the issue of excessive fees in the recent case of *Krinsk v. Fund Asset Management, Inc. (Krinsk)*.[84] Relying on the authority of *Gartenberg I* and *Schuyt*, the District Court determined that there are five relevant factors to consider when examining fees:

1. The expertise of the individual trustees of a fund, whether they are fully informed about all facts bearing on the adviser-manager's services and fee, and the extent of care and conscientiousness with which they perform their duties
2. The nature and quality of services provided to fund shareholders
3. The adviser's cost in providing these services
4. Economies of scale realized by the adviser as the fund grows larger
5. The volume of orders that must be processed by the fund's adviser [85]

This court also held that comparisons with other advisory fees do not satisfy the test under Section 36(b), since there is very little competition at the adviser level.[86]

Krinsk, however, entailed unique circumstances since the fund was part of Merrill Lynch's Cash Management Account program, which provided a number of intermediary services, including a traditional brokerage account, a savings vehicle

---

[83] Ibid., 979.

[84] *Krinsk v. Fund Asset Management, Inc., et al.*, U.S. District Court, S.D.N.Y., 85 Civ. 8428 (JMW) (June 27, 1988).

[85] Ibid., 30.

[86] Ibid., 30.

consisting of one of three money market accounts, a VISA card, check-writing, and a monthly statement. The court determined that the nature of the program was a "surrounding circumstance" to be considered when evaluating the fund's fee level. This was important for an examination of the costs and benefits of the fund to Merrill Lynch and to the fund's shareholders. Nonetheless, the court noted that the primary issue of the case was whether Merrill Lynch breached its fiduciary duty with respect to the fund *per se* in the advisory fees it received.

The court once again based its decision not on any economic analysis, nor on consideration of competition, but rather on the requirement that the plaintiff prove that the defendant did not meet its fiduciary responsibility. The court concluded that the plaintiff failed to meet his burden of proof and dismissed all claims. The analysis of the court revealed that the profitability the fund derived from fee-based activities was not outside the realm of reasonableness; there was no evidence to support the claim that economies of scale were present; both fees and expenses were within the normal industry range; and the trustees were qualified, well-informed, conscientious,[87] and careful in their deliberations approving the advisory fee.

Having discussed the post-1970 litigation involving money market funds, it is illuminating to examine which funds have been sued and, for the year before each suit began, what they have in common with one another. Table 3.3 describes the market share, yield, expense ratios, and respective rankings in these categories for each fund whose fees have been challenged.[88] A majority of these funds ranked in the top half of the industry with respect to net yield, despite their allegedly excessive fees. The expense ratios of the funds involved in litigation were not systematically greater than those for the industry generally. In fact, in the case of more than half of the

---

[87] Ibid., 72.

[88] In instances where the information was not available for a given year, data were used for the next closest year.

Table 3.3

Money Market Mutual Funds Involved in Excessive Fee Litigation After the 1970 Amendments

Fund name	Adviser	Year suit first filed	Assets[a] Year	Assets[a] % Share	Assets[a] Rank	Yield[a] % Share	Yield[a] Rank	Expense ratio[b] Year	Expense ratio[b] % Share	Expense ratio[b] Rank
Alliance Capital Reserves	Alliance Capital Mgmt. Corp.		1979	1.0	17/47	10.12	36/47	1980	0.80	34/45
Daily Income Fund	Daily Income Fund Inc.		1978	1.7	14/35	6.93	21/35	1979	0.74	19/32
Fidelity Daily Inc. Trust	Fidelity Mgmt. & Research Co.	1976	1978	12.5	3/35	7.40	3/35	1978	0.62	6/24
Liquid Assets Fund	The Dreyfus Corp.	1976	1978	13.0	2/35	6.81	26/35	1978	0.68	9/24
InterCapital Liquid Assets	Dean Witter Reynolds	1979	1978	6.5	5/35	7.25	8/35	1978	0.76	12/24
ML Ready Asset Trust	Merrill Lynch Asset Mgmt.	1979	1978	24.2	1/35	7.24	9/35	1978	0.74	11/24
CMA Money Trust	Merrill Lynch Asset Mgmt.	1980	1980	5.2	5/62	11.85	30/62	1980	NA	
Moneymart Assets	Adm: Bache Halsey Stuart Sheilds Adv: Cont'l Ill. Nat'l Bank	1980	1979	3.5	9/47	10.44	16/47	1980	0.62	16/45
Oppenheimer Money Mkt Fund	Oppenheimer Mgmt. Corp.	1980	1979	1.0	18/47	10.64	6/47	1979	0.65	9/32
Paine Webber Cashfund	Adm: Paine Webber Adv: Provident Inst'l Mgmt. Corp.	1980	1979	4.9	7/47	10.21	32/47	1980	0.60	11/45
Price Prime Reserve	T. Rowe Price Associates	1980	1979	2.3	11/47	10.64	6/47	1979	0.68	13/32
Reserve Fund	Reserve Mgmt. Corp.	1980	1979	5.6	6/47	10.67	5/47	1981	0.76	42/70
Shearson Daily Dividends	Adm: The Dreyfus Corp. Adv: Shearson/American Express	1980	1980	4.0	8/62	12.29	21/62	1980	0.60	13/45
Temporary Investment Fund	Adm: Shearson/American Express Adv: Provident Inst'l Mgmt. Corp.	1980	NA			NA		NA		

continued on next page

Table 3.3 continued

Fund name	Adviser	Year suit first filed	Assets[a]			Yield[a]		Expense ratio[b]		
			Year	% Share	Rank	% Share	Rank	Year	% Share	Rank
Cash Reserve Mgmt.	Adm: E.F. Hutton Adv: Morgan Guaranty Trust	1981	1980	5.4	4/62	12.70%	4/62	1980	0.49	4/45
Delaware Cash Reserves	Delaware Mgmt. Co.	1981	1980	1.1	21/62	12.46	10/62	1980	0.69	24/45
Fidelity Cash Reserves	Fidelity Mgmt. & Research Co.	1981	1980	1.7	16/62	12.23	25/62	1980	0.98	40/45
National Liquid Reserves	Nat'l Securities & Research Corp.	1981	1980	2.6	12/62	11.90	45/62	1980	0.69	25/45
NRTA/AARP US Gov. M. Market	Federated Investors Corp.	1981	1981	2.4	12/85	15.84	78/85	1981	0.99	63/70
Scudder Cash Investment Tr.	Scudder, Stevens & Clark	1981	1980	1.1	22/62	12.17	29/62	1980	0.80	35/45
Webster Cash Reserve	Adm: The Dreyfus Corp. Adv: Webster Mgmt. Corp.	1981	1980	1.0	23/62	12.06	36/62	1981	0.65	21/70
Daily Cash Accumulation	Oppenheimer Asset Mgmt. Corp.	1982	1981	3.7	7/85	17.58	4/85	1980	0.67	22/45
Lehman Cash Mgmt. Fund	Lehman Mgmt. Co. Inc.	1984	1983	0.5	41/189	8.88	30/189	1983	0.70	40/126
Cash Equivalent Fund	Kemper Financial Services	1985	1984	3.2	6/206	10.42	21/206	1984	0.72	48/167

Notes: [a]Rank is (fund ranking)/(total number of funds in that year).
[b]Expense ratio year corresponds to funds with a fiscal year ending between 12/31 and 11/30. Number of funds per year for performance indicators and expense ratio do not match because of differing data sources.

Source: Table 3.2; Lipper — Directors' Analytical Data (February, 1979-1985); Donoghue's Mutual Funds Almanac (1982).

funds for which this information is available, expense ratios were below the median ratio in the pertinent year. Here, it is worth noting that four of the eight funds whose expense ratios did exceed the median were ranked in the top half of the industry with respect to net yield. Not surprisingly, the table shows that suits have been brought predominantly against the largest MMFs in the industry. For example, in 1978, four of the top five funds were sued. By 1982, the fees of 20 of the top 25 ranking MMFs had been challenged.

This immediately raises the question of why smaller funds appear to be insulated from legal actions based on the 1940 Act. A likely explanation lies in the widespread belief that economies of scale are present. Since the failure of the adviser to share the benefits of the alleged economies of scale derived from increasing size of assets has been a primary issue in many cases, it is not surprising that the fees of advisers of smaller funds have not been subject to legal inquiry.

SUMMARY OF ECONOMIC ANALYSIS UTILIZED IN LITIGATION

With the exception of the District Court in the first Gartenberg case, the courts have either failed altogether to consider or have placed only minimum weight on the competitive characteristics of the mutual fund industry or other economic factors in trying cases alleging excessive advisory fees. In the appeal of *Gartenberg I*, the courts explicitly rejected the relevance for shareholders of competition among funds because of what they claim to be the general insensitivity of shareholders to the level of management fees. In general, judicial opinions have been based on the failure to prove any breach of fiduciary responsibility on the part of the plaintiff. There are, however, two areas in which the courts have utilized some form of economic or financial analysis to assist in identifying a possible breach of fiduciary duty. The two areas are economies of scale and the level of adviser profitability.

Despite numerous claims that economies of scale derive from increases in fund assets, no plaintiff has been able to produce evidence of the existence of economies of scale. Rather, the perception that they exist has been folklore in the industry. The District Court's view in *Gartenberg I* was somewhat different. This court acknowledged that economies of scale may exist up to a certain point beyond which transactions-based expenses dominate:

> While the unit costs of portfolio management and general administrative services have almost certainly declined as the Fund has grown, the far greater costs of providing shareholder services appear to have remained relatively stable.[89]

In *Krinsk*, the plaintiff attempted to establish economies of scale through an exhibit that showed that the ratio of fee-based expenses to fee-based revenues declined as the fund's asset size increased. The court appropriately concluded that this analysis did not indicate the presence of economies of scale *per se* and that detailed analysis examining unit costs would have to be performed. This conclusion, however, does not resolve the issue. Since the concept of scale economies grows ambiguous for a mutual fund complex offering several funds, it is not surprising that definitive evidence has not been produced.

The courts have also examined the profitability of an adviser-manager with respect to fee-based activities of a fund. The level of profitability of the adviser has been considered important evidence by the courts in determining whether fees are excessive. Since fees are a primary source of revenue for advisers, the courts have reasoned that excess profits would be earned if an adviser charged excessive fees. The courts' standard for determining whether the level of profitability is excessive is that profits must be so great as not to be the reasonable product of arm's-length bargaining between two independent parties with alternatives. The courts have been very hesitant to interfere with the board of directors' business

---

[89] *Gartenberg* 1981, 1055.

judgment, or with any decisions made with full disclosure of all material facts.

Although the courts' standard for judging the level of profitability is sound, they have not recognized the difficulties in isolating the profits associated with one fund among several in a complex. The courts have adopted fully distributed cost approaches for allocation of the joint and common costs incurred by the mutual fund complex. Yet, it is widely recognized that this method produces arbitrary results, which are dependent on the choice of allocation conventions. The different conventions can yield profit figures that vary significantly. Nonetheless, the courts have rejected other costs, such as incremental and marginal costs, claiming that they fail to reflect the true cost of a product, since they do not include any shared costs arising from joint production.

APPENDIX

Difficulty of Testing Whether Profits of a Single Product are Excessive in a Multiproduct Firm

The adviser of a money market mutual fund is almost always a multiproduct enterprise. Because most funds are part of a complex of investment outlets, each adviser of such a complex is responsible for the administration of each of the component funds and other entities. The advice provided to each such entity must, for reasons that will be clearer presently, be considered a separate product of the adviser firm. In addition, many advisers provide services such as brokerage, insurance, etc. Our study of the industry indicates that, on the average, an advisory firm provides approximately three such separate broad product categories.

The fact that an enterprise produces a multiplicity of products creates great difficulties for the provision of defensible and pertinent evidence to test a claim that the firm earns excessive profits from or charges excessive prices for one of its products. Aside from the basic difficulty of deciding upon the borderline between reasonable and excessive prices, there is the near-universal difficulty of dealing with costs that are incurred in common on behalf of two or more of the company's products. Outlays on company accounting, for example, may serve all of the firm's products simultaneously. The time spent on telephone calls with customers who want to switch money from fund A to fund B in the same complex obviously is an outlay necessary for the operation of *both* these funds. Many other examples of such common costs are easily provided. They are obviously present and it is easy to demonstrate that they are substantial.[90]

The difficulty caused by such common costs is that while we know how much they amount to in total, there is no way of

---

[90] Activities common to all funds in a single complex include, for example, investor communications and shareholder accounting.

determining what portion of such a common cost is legitimately attributable to *any* particular one of the products on whose behalf it is incurred. If the wage and other costs of telephone operations devoted to switching money (in either direction between funds A and B, in our previous example) is $10 million per year, how much of this is to be ascribed to A and how much to B? Half and half? Even if the bulk of its funds went to A, or if B is the larger fund by far, or if the nature of B makes its cost of operations much higher than A's? Economists generally agree that such questions are unanswerable and even meaningless. The cost is incurred on behalf of *both* funds, and that is all that is legitimately possible to show. By definition, such costs are not divisible on any economically substantive criterion, and many rules for dividing them up among the various products on whose behalf they are incurred must inescapably be based on some arbitrarily selected bookkeeping rule that can readily be replaced with a dozen other such rules, any one of them no more arbitrary than the first. The trouble is that any one such rule will attribute to a given company product X a different share of the total common cost than is assigned to it by any other rule.

It is easy to see the resulting difficulty for determination of the profitability of product X. Suppose X's revenues to the supplier of the product are $1 million, after deduction of the directly attributable (i.e., noncommon) costs of X. If arbitrary criterion A assigns $800,000 of common costs to X, then that product will be said to have earned $200,000 in profit. On the other hand, if another rule for subdivision of the firm's costs assigns only $300,000 of those costs to X, it will apparently follow that the profits of X were $700,000. Which is the correct figure? Economists agree that *neither* of them is. Obviously, the methods for dealing with the profitability of a particular product in a multiproduct firm require further examination. Accordingly, the different approaches that have been used for the purpose will be examined next.

First, however, a bit must be said about what is generally accepted as the borderline between reasonable and excessive profits. As in all such matters, the competitive market standard is widely accepted here, and has been used in various fields of regulation by courts, regulatory agencies, and economists. The basic premise is that a highly competitive industry cannot earn excessive profits for any substantial period of time because, if it were to do so, the opportunity to share in the high earning would rapidly attract new entrants, whose addition to industry output levels would quickly force down prices and profits.

Accordingly, it is generally agreed that a company's total profits are judged excessive if and only if over a longer period they exceed the prevailing competitive rate of return.[91] That is, the profits of a firm are not excessive if and only if, on the average (i.e., averaging periods of favorable and unfavorable business conditions), those profits, calculated as a percentage of the total amount of capital the owners have tied up in the enterprise, do not exceed the returns currently earned in the economy (on the average) by competitive firms comparable in riskiness to the enterprise in question. This, then, is the criterion that a court, a regulatory agency, or an outside trustee should use to evaluate the total profits earned by a money market mutual fund's advisory firm.

But this has not usually been the problem with which the courts have had to grapple. Instead, the task that has fallen to them has been to determine whether the fee the adviser charges to *a particular* money market mutual fund X is too high, or whether the profit the adviser derives from X is excessive. And these matters cannot escape the multiproduct problems described earlier in this section. Those problems must be faced explicitly, and defensible methods designed to deal with the issue must be designed specially. We therefore turn next to the approaches that have been devised for this purpose.

---

[91] One important exception must be noted. Firms with a record of successful innovation should be expected to earn more than competitive profits. This is the incentive that induces firms to take the risks and bear the costs of the innovation process. Even in very competitive markets, innovative firms earn such high returns (temporarily) with the aid of the lower costs or of the superior products yielded by their innovations.

The Fully Allocated Cost Approach.   A procedure frequently resorted to by regulators in dealing with the problems that have just been described, at least until recently, is called *fully allocated cost* or *fully distributed cost*. Full-cost allocation is a procedure widely used for accounting purposes. It is employed for multiproduct firms to obtain something that is believed to approximate the true average costs of the enterprise's individual products. In essence, its procedure is to start from the figure for the total costs incurred by the firm during the period at issue, and somehow to divide those costs up among the individual products. That is, each such product is assigned its own fully allocated cost figure, calculated in such a way that the sum of those individual figures yields a total precisely equal to the total costs of the enterprise.   Each product's fully allocated cost number is then divided by the quantity of that product's output, to yield a per-unit allocated cost that is presumed to have some pertinence for the appropriate price of that product, and to serve as an indicator of its profitability.

The basic difficulty inherent in this procedure, as was already indicated, is that there exists no unique way having any economic justification of dividing the firm's total costs among its products.   Typically, substantial outlays will have been incurred in common on behalf of several of the firm's products. These common outlays can only be divided up among the products they serve on the basis of some admittedly arbitrary accounting convention. The cliche illustration is the salary of the firm's chief executive officer, which can only be apportioned among its products by some leap of faith. But there are, of course, many other items in the budget of the modern enterprise that share this characteristic. As a result, it is generally conceded, even by those who defend their use, that fully allocated figures are ultimately arbitrary.

What remains misleading in these concessions is the implied conclusion that while fully allocated cost figures calculated on the basis of different (but equally arbitrary) accounting conventions, though they will differ from one another, will probably all approximate one another to a reasonable degree. Therefore, whichever convention happens to be selected can with some degree of confidence be accepted as a valid estimate of some underlying average cost. Such a conclusion turns out to be completely false. Below it is shown, both on the basis of economic analysis and with the aid of real data for an actual firm, that a change in the basis of allocation can modify the resulting fully allocated cost figures so dramatically that for any particular product, what appeared to be a price that yielded a profit of several hundred percent (!) under one reasonable-appearing calculation is reduced to a loss of comparable magnitude under another.

With fully allocated cost figures inherently so arbitrary and so unrelated to any economic analysis pertinent to what can be referred to as *cost causation*, it follows that these numbers cannot pretend to have any fixed relation to the prices that will emerge under competitive market conditions, or to the prices that will most effectively serve the interests of the general public. Regulation of rates on the basis of fully allocated costs inevitably becomes an exercise in random behavior, with nothing but some appearance of rationality being preserved. If the figures are arbitrary, and if their magnitudes are subject to substantial modification by changes among the available and equally (in)defensible calculation procedures, any prices calculated on the basis of such numbers must be comparably arbitrary, and unrelated to any reasonably regulatory goals.

This does not mean, incidentally, that it is desirable for a regulator to fix prices *exclusively* on the basis of cost information alone so long as the cost datum used for the purpose is more defensible than fully allocated cost. We know that in free markets the prices of firms whose production process is not characterized by perfectly constant returns to scale will be influenced by both cost and demand conditions. Whatever the pertinent cost concept, it is clear that if some development decreases costs in a competitive market, prices are sure to have to follow. But at different times and for different products, the relationship between prices and costs will vary in competitive markets depending on the pertinent demand conditions. To take an obvious example, everyone knows that in times when business conditions are unpropitious as a result of slack demand, competitive prices are apt to be very low relative to the pertinent costs, with the firm expecting to make up for any resulting shortfall in periods when demands are more favorable. In other words, any price regulation that bases limits on prices exclusively on some cost calculation, without leaving any scope for a role by demand conditions (as is typically true of the fully allocated cost regulatory processes), necessarily conflicts with the behavior of competitive markets. Here, without intending to do so, the regulation acts so as to constrain the pricing process to a degree beyond that which would be imposed by competitive market conditions. The regulation then restricts business decision making in a way that cannot be justified as part of the obligation of a regulator to serve as a substitute for competition in markets where the power of competition is deemed inadequate.

One noteworthy paradox of full-cost price regulation is that while it is explicitly designed to ensure adequate revenues to the regulated firm, in fact it very often prevents that firm from earning enough to cover all its costs, including its cost of capital. This observation may be surprising, but it is easy to demonstrate. The paradox, of course, arises from the fact that under most if not all types of full-cost rate regulation, each rate is allowed to equal the corresponding fully allocated cost figure, so that the revenues from each product are permitted in each period to equal the product's fully allocated cost. In consequence, the firm's total revenues are then necessarily *permitted* to equal its total costs, which are equal to the sum of fully allocated costs.

How then, can it conceivably be possible under such a regime for the firm to be prevented by regulation from covering all its costs? The answer is that there is usually a large gap between what the regulator permits the firm to do and what the market allows. The regulator may permit a product to be sold at a price of $50, but if no one wants to pay that price for the product there is nothing the regulator can (or should) do about it. Since demand conditions are systematically disregarded by full-cost pricing rules, it is virtually certain that, for the different products of the regulated firm, some of the prices that emerge from the regulatory process will be below those that are called for by current demand conditions while others will be above the levels appropriate in light of the current state of demand. The firm will obviously fall behind its revenue goals in those markets in which the regulatory price figure is higher than demand conditions permit. But the firm will be precluded from making up for the shortfall in its remaining markets, where regulation holds prices below the levels called for by demands. The same problem also arises intertemporally. If prices are governed by fully allocated costs alone both in periods when demand is substantial and when it is very limited, the firm will be condemned by regulation to lose money in the latter type of periods when markets are depressed, and the enterprise will be precluded by regulation from compensating for that shortfall in periods when market conditions are better. The net result, all too often, is that full-cost regulation degenerates into a device that inadvertently but effectively precludes the regulated firm from earning all the revenues it needs to be able to serve its customers' current and future needs effectively.

One must conclude that fully allocated cost methods of rate regulation are based on figures that are totally arbitrary and that cannot be protected from manipulation, inadvertent or deliberate; that the process systematically impedes the firm in its attempts to cover its total costs and may well preclude it from doing so; and, above all, that by excluding demand conditions from playing their proper role in the pricing process, the full-cost rate regulation procedures divorce themselves from the competitive market model and so yield a structure of prices that does not best serve the interests of the general public. It is for such reasons that leading economists are unanimous in their opposition to this regulatory approach.

In recent years regulatory commissions and the courts have also recognized increasingly the deficiencies of the fully allocated cost procedures. More and more, they are seeking and adopting more defensible substitutes. Where fully allocated cost procedures continue to be used, they tend to be employed only as general guides, and they are used for that purpose because traditional accounting practice has made it relatively easy and routine to calculate such costs.

The Use of Price Caps and Price Floors. An alternative approach to regulation of the prices of a multiproduct firm, one advocated by a number of economists, follows the competitive market model as a guide for regulation. That is, it works on the premise that the proper role of regulation is to serve as a substitute for competition in those markets where competition is deemed inadequate to protect consumer interests sufficiently.

Here, the procedure takes account of the fact that the competitive market model calls for regulatory adoption of both a lower and an upper bound upon prices. Within those bounds, it is suggested, the firm should be left free to select its prices in accord with its normally superior knowledge of the demand conditions that face it. But the regulator's legitimate task in the normal oversight of the pricing process is to ensure that the prices set by the firm do not go below the appropriate floor or exceed the appropriate ceiling. Where production is characterized by constant returns to scale, prices equal to marginal costs yield revenues that just cover total costs, as the standard analysis of economic textbooks demonstrates. But where some form of scale economies is present, so that prices equal to marginal costs must yield total revenues that fall short of total costs, other pricing rules must apply, and then the competitive floors and ceilings will normally differ from one another.

If the ceilings on prices adopted by regulation are based on the behavior of competitive markets, they will clearly rule out excessive profits. The reason should be obvious. One of the well-recognized virtues of effective competition is the fact that it precludes excessive profit by making any market in which excessive prices are imposed attractive and vulnerable to competitive entry, which will soon enough deprive the misbehaving firm of its customers. If regulatory price ceilings prevent the firm from charging prices that it could not sustain under effectively competitive conditions, it follows that the regulated firm, equally with the competitive firm, then will be prevented from earning any excess profits.

Let us see next how economic analysis indicates that the floor levels and those ceiling levels for regulated prices ought to be selected. Let us first deal with the principles for the determination of floors. Here, as in the determination of ceilings, the competitive market model serves as the economists' guide. This model tells us that the proper floor under the price of some product is its per-unit incremental cost, where the incremental cost of a product X is defined as the firm's current total cost for all its products together, minus the lower total cost that the firm would incur if it ceased production of X altogether. The reason that the per-unit incremental cost of X (i.e., the incremental cost of X divided by the output of X) is the appropriate floor is straightforward. In an effectively competitive market, where ease of entry rules out any incentive for predatory price behavior, no firm will ever find it in its interest to sell any product at any price below the pertinent incremental cost, because that means that the sales bring in revenues lower than the cost that they cause. Thus, in competitive markets, prices will never fall below incremental costs. But in such a market prices may sometimes be set, quite legitimately, very close to the corresponding incremental costs, so long as these prices are slightly above those costs. This is so because such sales, by definition, make a positive profit contribution, since their revenues (slightly) exceed the cost added by the sales. If demand conditions happen to permit no more favorable pricing terms for such sales, the firm is well advised to go ahead with them nevertheless — since a small but positive profit contribution is better than none.

In sum, incremental cost is a legitimate competitive floor under prices, because no lower price can serve a defensible business purpose. It has also just been shown that no price floor higher than incremental cost is generally acceptable, because prices very close to incremental costs can be entirely legitimate, and are not precluded by competitive market forces.

Before turning to the way in which ceilings on prices should be determined, it is appropriate to offer an observation on the role of ceilings, one that may be somewhat illuminating here and that will play a crucial role later in this discussion. There is a theorem in the economics literature (the proof will be provided presently) that tells us the following: If a regulator ensures that the firm whose prices are being supervised does not earn excessive profits overall, and that one of its prices is set below its proper floor, then it follows tautologically that one of those prices can be excessive. That is, the theorem tells us than an *overall* earning test and a *floor* test for individual prices are all that is required. Once these tests are passed, a supplementary comparison of prices and price *ceilings* is redundant.

Why is this so? To see this, consider a case in which none of the firm's prices is inadequate, and in which, in addition, some of these prices are excessive. Then it follows that the firm's overall earnings must be excessive, that is, that the excessiveness of some of its prices would be revealed by the test of the excessiveness of the firm's overall earnings. Put another way, if the firm's overall earnings are not excessive, then if some of its products are contributing excessive revenues, it follows tautologically that those indefensibly high earnings must be offset by inadequate earnings of other products. Thus, excessive earnings on any product or group of products must show up either as excessive overall earnings or as inadequate earnings from some particular products. That is why if the firm passes both the test of absence of excessive overall earnings and the test that checks whether any of its individual product prices is inadequate, a supplementary test comparing prices and their ceilings is rendered unnecessary.

Let us now go on to describe what economic analysis indicates about the determination of legitimate price ceilings. Here, too, the competitive model is used as the guide, and it indicates that the ceiling should be set at the level of what has been called stand-alone cost. A price or a set of prices is defined to exceed the stand-alone cost of the products to which it applies if it yields revenues that exceed the costs that would be incurred by an entrant producing the same bundle of products in a hypothetical market in which entry was completely unimpeded but which was in every other respect identical with the market actually in question. We know that where entry is unimpeded such prices cannot be sustained, while prices even only slightly lower than that may be able to persist because they attract no new competition. Thus, the competitive market model tells us that these entry-inducing prices — prices equal to stand-alone costs — are the proper price ceilings for regulation to adopt. This is so because these ceilings ensure that purchasers of regulated products receive all the price protection that absolute freedom of entry, as the epitome of competitiveness (in the presence of scale economics), would provide to them.

Does a Particular Product Yield Excess Profit? Having described the method called for by economic analysis to test whether the *price* of some product in a multiproduct firm is too high, we turn, finally, to the corresponding test to determine whether the profit contribution of a product line or division of a multiproduct firm is or is not excessive. The method, in summary, involves two steps: (1) calculating the overall rate of return of the entire enterprise to determine whether it is or is not excessive, and (2) checking whether or not each and every one of its product lines is making a net contribution toward recovery of fixed and common costs. If both tests are passed, it follows that no product line can be yielding excessive profits.

The first issue raised by this brief recapitulation of this profit-testing procedure is how one measures whether a product line is making at least the minimum net contribution required. The answer is identical with the price-floor test that has already been described, comparing the revenues and the incremental costs of the product in question. Since the incremental cost of some product X can be interpreted as the expense *caused* by the production of X, it follows that if the revenue contributed by that product line exceeds the costs that it caused, i.e., if that revenue exceeds X's incremental cost, then X must be making a net contribution toward recovery of the firm's fixed and common costs.

Now, as has already been argued intuitively, and will presently be proved, if a firm earns, overall, a competitive rate of return on its capital, and if the product lines (other than X) of the firm bring in a revenue at least equal to their incremental cost, then it is impossible for the remaining product line X to be priced excessively and, hence, to earn profits in excess of what that product line could contribute in a competitive market. For with other product lines providing at least a minimum acceptable revenue, if the remaining line brought in an excessive revenue, the company as a whole would inevitably be earning profits in excess of the competitive standard, something that the first portion of the excessive profits test already will have investigated.

This concludes an intuitive discussion of the proposition that underlies the test determining whether or not the profits of some particular product are excessive. To prove formally that the two-part test is sufficient to determine whether the profit of any one of the firm's products is excessive, we use the following notation.

Let

x = the quantity of the product whose profits and prices are under examination

y = the vector of quantities of the other outputs of the firm

$C(x, y)$ = the total cost of producing the current outputs of these products

Rx = the revenue the firm derives from sale of x

Then, obviously $C(x, y) - C(x, 0)$ is the incremental cost of y and $C(x, 0)$ is the stand-alone cost of X. Consequently, the profits from the sale of x can be defined to pass the stand-alone cost test if

$$Rx \leq C(x, 0),$$

i.e., if no specialized entrant can afford to supply x on terms more favorable to the customer.

To prove our result that this is guaranteed by passage of the two-part test, let us assume that both parts of the test are indeed passed. Then total revenue of x and aggregate product y must just be sufficient to cover their total cost (including a competitive return to capital), i.e.,

$$Rx + Ry = C (x, y).$$

Moreover, if the revenues from the sale of product vector y cover its incremental cost, then

$$Ry \geq C (x, y) - C (x, 0).$$

Subtracting this inequality from the previous equation, we immediately obtain the desired result,

$$Rx \leq C (x, 0).$$

In sum, to determine whether a particular product or service of a multiproduct firm is or is not overpriced or whether it does or does not yield excessive profits, one need not employ the discredited approach that relies on fully allocated cost. Instead, the two-part test that has just been described can provide a defensible answer. Thus, if it proves necessary to test whether an adviser is overcharging for the services to a particular fund, this is the test that recommends itself for the purpose.

FOUR

ANALYSIS OF THE ADVISER-SHAREHOLDER RELATIONSHIP IN THE MUTUAL FUND INDUSTRY

INTRODUCTION

The main attribute of mutual fund advisory services that makes them the subject of such extensive judicial and legal inquiry is the nature of the relationship between a mutual fund and the supplier of these services. The mutual fund and its adviser are not independent enterprises, since the mutual fund is the creation of the advisory enterprise. As a result, it may appear that there is no freedom to shop around and find the firm that is prepared to supply the advisory services on the most favorable financial terms. Proponents of industry regulation emphasize this feature of mutual funds, which, in their opinion, has permitted fund managers to charge excessive fees or otherwise engage in self-seeking behavior[92] at the expense of mutual fund shareholders.

The objective of this chapter is to identify the questions that must be resolved before one can assess the appropriateness of the legal remedies provided in the ICA. Several approaches to an analysis of the transactions between the shareholders and

---

[92] Self-seeking behavior here is taken to entail willingness by advisers to provide incomplete or distorted information and to make calculated efforts to mislead.

adviser of a mutual fund are described. Based on the application of these approaches, the chapters that follow seek to offer insights on the nature of the underlying adviser-shareholder relationship.

EXAMINATION OF ORGANIZATIONAL STRUCTURE

Shareholders and Advisers as Contracting Agents

What characterizes the transactions between shareholders of a mutual fund and its adviser? The literature dealing with the economics of contractual relationships provides one approach for answering this question.[93] Contract analysis focuses on the particular attributes of a transaction and the behavior of the individual parties to the transaction. This focus provides information about the types of contracts and enforcement mechanisms necessary to prevent either party to a transaction from engaging in self-seeking behavior. In addition to spelling out the terms, explicit contracts usually contain enforcement mechanisms designed to ensure that neither party to a transaction will unfairly take advantage of the other party. However, since contracting is costly, individuals typically choose to avoid entering into contractual relationships altogether if alternative enforcement mechanisms exist to bring about the desired behavior. For example, explicit contracts are likely to be unnecessary to enforce transactions in markets that are highly competitive because, with low transactions costs, market forces can be depended on to provide the necessary discipline.

---

[93] See Oliver E. Williamson, *The Economic Institutions of Capitalism* (New York: The Free Press, Macmillan, Inc., 1985); Benjamin Klein, R.A. Crawford, and A.A. Alchian, "Vertical Integration, Appropriable Rents, and the Competitive Contracting Process," *Journal of Law and Economics*, vol. 21 (October, 1978), 297-326; and Benjamin Klein, "Transaction Cost Determinants of 'Unfair' Contractual Arrangements," *American Economic Review*, vol. 70 (May, 1980), 356-362.

An analysis that interprets the role of the shareholders of a mutual fund and its adviser as that of contracting agents permits a dual assessment. First, it allows an assessment of the role of regulation in facilitating execution of the implicit contract between mutual fund shareholders and advisers. Second, it enables us to evaluate whether the organization of adviser-shareholder transactions is efficient in minimizing the transactions costs that inevitably arise in exchanges between the two parties.

A fundamental objective of contract analysis is to identify the most efficient and effective contracting process implied by the characteristics of a particular transaction. The attributes of primary concern are those that relate to the assumed behavior of the parties to the transaction and the nature of the investments undertaken by each party. Under a variety of conditions, successful execution of transactions will not be dependent on the presence of explicit contracts or on outside government regulation. These mechanisms are called for only when conditions are such that competition or implicit agreements fail to ensure that transactions are executed in a fair and efficient manner.[94] Consequently, one of the main goals of the discussion here is to determine an appropriate structure to govern transactions between shareholders and fund managers, given the behavior of each and the nature of the investments each party undertakes.

While it is clear from our earlier discussion that both courts and regulators habitually have imputed self-seeking behavior to mutual fund advisers, it does not necessarily follow that shareholder protection is required. Even if fund advisers disregard the interests of shareholders, competition may produce the market discipline necessary to protect shareholders' interests, particularly when factors restricting shareholder mobility are not present. Without constraints on the mobility of shareholders, the availability of market alternatives can effectively protect shareholders against self-interested decisions by fund advisers.

---

[94] Oliver E. Williamson, *The Economic Institutions of Capitalism,* op. cit.

To assess whether substantial financial damage to shareholders by mutual fund advisers is a real possibility, one must analyze the nature of mutual fund transactions. As discussed in Chapter One, a key feature in the evolution of the mutual fund industry has been the material increase in investor mobility following the shift away from illiquid closed-end funds to highly liquid open-end mutual funds. Before the adoption of the 1940 Act, closed-end funds were the primary offering of investment companies. Unlike open-end mutual funds, where the fund stands ready to sell and redeem shares contractually, investments in closed-end funds are redeemable only by trading in the marketplace.

The distinction between closed-end and open-end funds is critical for an analysis of the adviser-shareholder relationship. Given the thin market in which closed-end funds are traded and the frequently illiquid assets in which these funds invest, shareholders who invested in closed-end funds before the 1940 Act were in effect undertaking sunk investments in each transaction, which made them vulnerable to expropriation by fund managers. Front-end or back-end sales loads also contributed to the sunk nature of shareholder investments. The characteristics of adviser-shareholder transactions that may have been responsible for the abuses that led to the 1940 Act will be examined further below. In particular, the importance of the form of organization of mutual funds, focusing on such issues as whether the fund is closed-end or open-end, the differences in their load features, and their evolution since 1940 will be examined in Chapter Five.

While the 1940 Act was designed to protect shareholders against further abuse by fund advisers, the mutual fund industry has advanced considerably since that time. Whatever the merits of the regulatory remedy adopted in the Investment Company Act in 1940, one cannot presume that its merits remain unchanged in current circumstances. To evaluate the current merits of the 1940 Act, it is necessary to investigate the degree to which current industry practices discipline the behavior of mutual fund managers. In particular, it is necessary to study the extent to which no-load or low-load, open-end mutual funds constitute an efficient contractual remedy relative to the regulation of advisory fees.

Competition as a Restraining Force

We have seen that the potential for abusive behavior by mutual fund managers toward their shareholders can be examined by looking at the role of transactions costs and, in particular, whether they impede investor mobility. These same issues can also be examined with the aid of more traditional market analysis. Both approaches offer significant insights and provide support for one another's conclusions. However, while the focus of contractual analysis is on the presence of sunk investments associated with individual transactions, market analysis considers whether competition at the adviser level is sufficient to ensure that the fees charged by advisers will not exceed competitive levels.

The connection between fee-setting behavior and the level of competition is far from obvious, as repeated court opinions demonstrate. Nevertheless, it remains true that the presence of sufficiently strong competition among mutual fund advisers can be relied upon to prevent the overpricing of advisory services, despite the fact that individual funds are captives of their advisers, and that advisory fees are a relatively small element in the determination of a fund's yield. To see that competition is sufficient to prevent overpayment of fees to advisers, assume that the mutual fund market is highly competitive[95] and that, in particular, unrestricted entry opportunities are available to potential operators of mutual funds. The relevant inquiry then reduces to the following: Does there exist a source from which overpayments to the supplier of advisory services could be made? The answer is clearly no. Because the return to firms in competitive markets just equals the economic return associated with the activities they perform, no

---

[95] In reality, the degree of competition in this market is determined by a variety of influences that are discussed in detail in the following sections.

mutual fund in a competitive market can pay more than the going market rate for advisory services whether or not the supplier of advisory services operates at arm's-length from the input purchaser, i.e., the mutual fund.

Suppose that a mutual fund should agree to pay a greater price than the going market rate for advisory and management services, and the mutual fund attempts to finance that overpayment by lowering the return on its shareholders' investment. As long as the fund's shareholders react by quickly diverting their assets to other funds that are in a position to offer a higher rate of return (by virtue of the fact that they have not agreed to the overpayment to their fund advisers), the offending mutual fund will rapidly find itself excluded from the field of enterprise. Even in the extreme and implausible case in which all funds were to agree collusively to such an overpayment, newly entering advisers could create funds whose advisory fees did not contain an overpayment. As a result, incumbent funds and their advisers eventually would be replaced.

The ability of a mutual fund adviser to charge excess fees is independent of whether the fund and its adviser are affiliated or not. As long as shareholders are free to switch funds at little cost and will do so given small changes in relative net yield,[96] the structure of the adviser-fund relationship is irrelevant. Thus, the focus of the courts and policy-makers on the affiliated nature of the adviser-fund relationship has been misplaced. Shareholders' ability to transfer their assets as a function of net yield is the same regardless of whether the adviser is external to the firm, external to the fund, or internal to the fund. In such cases, competition in the product market determines the equilibrium price of the inputs to the fund, including advisory fees. Analyzed in terms of market dynamics, competition among mutual funds ensures that no overpayments will be made to a fund's adviser. Competition results in a

---

[96] Later evidence will be provided showing that investors do in fact switch in response to small differences in yields.

larger set of substitute investment opportunities, and low switching costs make such substitution occur easily.

The same conclusion holds when the feasibility of overpayment is analyzed in contractual rather than market terms. The unit of analysis in the contractual agreement is the transaction rather than the market as a whole. The focus is thus on the individual shareholder's investment decision and on the adviser's role in determining whether alternative vehicles are accessible to investors. Thus, no matter whether market analysis or a contractual approach is used, the availability of market alternatives ultimately provides shareholders adequate protection against self-interested behavior by advisers. In this sense, the two approaches to analyzing the adviser-shareholder relationship are not only consistent; they are themselves mutually reinforcing.

FIVE

A STUDY OF CURRENT MARKET CONDITIONS IN THE MUTUAL FUND INDUSTRY

INTRODUCTION

The purpose of this chapter is to determine whether the mutual fund industry is competitive and, therefore, whether the forces of competition are sufficient to restrain managers of mutual funds from behaving in a manner contrary to share-holders' interests. If competition prevents abuses, then regulation may not be warranted. In this chapter, we provide a framework for the evaluation of competition in the mutual fund industry.

THE ANALYTIC FRAMEWORK: ON INDUSTRY STRUCTURE, PERFORMANCE, AND CONDUCT

Economics literature provides carefully constructed standards for judging whether an industry can be relied upon automatically to perform in a way that serves the public interest most effectively or whether some form of intervention is required to protect that interest. Usually, concerns about such matters arise when the industry approximates a monopoly or appears to be an oligopoly dominated by a few powerful firms. However, no one can reasonably conclude that mutual funds or their advisers exhibit such characteristics. There simply are too many of them, their rivalry is too obvious, and their entry record is too substantial for this hypothesis to be tenable. Thus, while some of the standard analysis of the relation between structure and conduct will be reviewed here, we will also address other issues pertinent to the analytical foundations of our study.

First, it will be necessary to distinguish between what may be referred to as *performance* and *conduct*. Second, it will be necessary to talk about the relation between efficiency and pricing performance in final outputs and their counterparts for the use of *inputs* needed to provide the final products.

With regard to the first of these matters, we will, in accord with normal usage in the literature of economics, consider the mutual fund industry's performance to be exemplary if

1. Given the current state of technology, the operations of mutual funds are carried out as efficiently as possible (i.e., at as low a total cost as is attainable, with the current levels of its outputs)

2. The industry prices its products in a competitive manner, meaning that a reduction in any of its prices will prevent some pertinent cost from being covered

Thus, efficiency and competitive pricing are what is meant by good performance.

In contrast, even when *performance* in that narrow sense is quite acceptable, conduct may be unacceptable in the sense that suppliers may provide inadequate or misleading information to consumers or may engage in outright fraud or product misrepresentation. We will see that the very market structures usually accepted as the most effective guarantors of good performance of any industry may be the poorest from the point of view of enforcement of good conduct — something not universally recognized in economics literature. It is precisely for this reason that this study will recommend for mutual funds a substantial reduction of the sort of regulations that are usually employed to improve performance; but we will emphatically *not* recommend any weakening of the disclosure rules that help to ensure good conduct.

The input-pricing issue assumes special importance for this study because advisory services must be interpreted, for analytic purposes, as the provision of a bundle of the inputs needed for a mutual fund to supply its products to final consumers. Just as a conventional television set cannot be made without transistors, electric wire, a few screws, etc., a mutual fund cannot operate without the investment decisions, communications services, and record keeping supplied by the advisory firm.

Now, the fundamental issue that has been raised by critics of the operations of mutual funds and their advisers is whether the advisers' services to the funds are overpriced because a fund is unable to shop around for advisers with lower prices. Accordingly, it will be necessary to examine whether there are any market structures for final *out*puts that can be relied upon to rule out such undesirable performance in input pricing. In particular, it will be necessary to study, if such desirable structural forms exist, whether they characterize the mutual funds industry in reality. We will conclude that such types of industry structure do in fact exist and that they typify the mutual funds as a group.

PERFECT COMPETITION AND PERFECT CONTESTABILITY AS THEORETICAL STRUCTURAL IDEALS

It is generally recognized that strong competition is the instrument of the market mechanism that ensures good performance in the sense just defined. In particular, there are two forms of industry structure that constitute theoretical ideals of highly effective competition, even though they are likely only to be approximated, at best, in a limited number of industries in reality. These industry forms guarantee that production will be carried out efficiently, and that neither prices nor profits will be excessive.

Perfect competition is defined by the textbooks as the structure of an industry in which (1) all firms are so small in terms of outputs and assets as to constitute a negligible share of those of the industry, (2) the products produced by different firms are identical (product homogeneity), and (3) there are no impediments to entry and exit. This is the standard textbook ideal of competition, but it is an industry form that can never be found in any field of endeavor in which the nature of technology is such as to provide scale economies. For where such economies are available, by definition, large firms will be more efficient than small ones, so that the tiny enterprises that are the hallmark of perfect competition will not be able to survive. Indeed, their survival would hardly benefit consumers in these circumstances, since prices would then have to be raised sufficiently to cover the high costs of small-scale production.

Where perfect competition is out of the question, an alternative theoretical ideal remains available, that of *perfect contestability*. This refers to a case in which, whether firms are large or small, new firms can enter or exit without restriction and *without incurring any sunk costs*. That is, any firm which enters, even if it must make a large investment in order to open for business, can recoup that investment without loss or delay if it decides to leave. For example, to run a barge line on the lower Mississippi a firm must invest in barges and tow boats. However, if business conditions prove more promising on the Ohio, it is easy and virtually costless to withdraw that investment from the one geographic area and move it to the other.

It should now be obvious how contestability precludes excessive profits, prices, and inefficiency alike. Excessive profits on the Ohio will attract barge operators from elsewhere, whose entry will rapidly depress prices and profits. Similarly, inefficient barge-line operators in one area will be vulnerable to incursions by more efficiently run barge lines from elsewhere. Thus, the market will chastise poorly run or greedy firms, at least where something like perfect contestability, with its ease of entry and exit, prevails. This, along with perfect competition, is the theoretical ideal, so far as industry *performance* is concerned, and that explains why these industry structures are used so often as guides in the analysis of regulatory policy, as has been done for industries such as air and rail transportation and telecommunications.

INDUSTRY CONCENTRATION

Where entry barriers are present, concern over market concentration may well be warranted. If entry barriers exist, most markets characterized by few sellers or by few buyers are likely to perform poorly. Where seller concentration is high, prices and profits may tend to exceed the competitive levels, and product quality may also be relatively low. In such circumstances, decreases in concentration generally result in intensification of competition that moves prices, output, and product quality toward competitive levels.

The concentration level is measured in relation to a relevant market. A market that is defined too narrowly will overstate concentration, while a market defined too broadly is likely to do just the opposite. The definition of the relevant market is not concise. In theory, the relevant market includes all close substitutes. In identifying these substitutes, two economic concepts are pertinent: demand substitutability and supply substitutability. The first refers to the willingness of consumers to buy one product instead of another when the relative price of the latter is increased. Supply substitutability refers to the ability of producers to respond to an increase in the relative price of a product by devoting new or additional production capacity to the product whose price has increased. Thus, a relevant market must include (1) firms that currently produce the identical set of competing products, (2) firms that produce close-substitute products, and (3) firms that currently do not produce the competing product but could do so within a reasonable time frame. In reality, however, since the degree of closeness of products lies along a continuum, it is impossible to define precise boundaries.

In applying these concepts to the present matter, it is clear that mutual funds are only a portion of the relevant market. Fluctuations in the total assets invested in mutual funds as actual and expected returns vary indicate that investors are switching their assets into different types of investments. This behavior is exactly what is meant by demand-side substitutability. It is precisely those products whose demand increases as a direct result of a decline in the demand for mutual funds that should be included in the relevant market. On the supply side, many types of firms not currently providing mutual fund services could quickly supply these services if the fees charged by mutual fund advisers were to rise above competitive levels. The sponsors of mutual funds have come from all types of financial intermediaries, which demonstrates the lack of specialized knowledge or assets required to enter the industry.

While it is clear that the relevant market includes not only existing mutual fund managers, but also other financial intermediaries that are potential sources of supply, our analysis of concentration is confined to existing mutual fund advisers. Thus, the relevant market is even less concentrated than the data presented below suggest. However, even within this restrictive market assumption, the level of concentration does not warrant concern.

To estimate the degree of concentration in the mutual fund industry, one can use either of the two generally accepted measures: concentration ratios or the Herfindahl-Hirschman Index (HHI). The latter is calculated by summing the squared market shares of all funds in the market.[97] HHIs range on a scale from zero to 10,000. The larger the HHI, the more concentrated is the market. The Department of Justice Merger Guidelines describe a market with an HHI greater than 1,800 as "highly concentrated," one with an HHI between 1,000 and

---

[97] For example, if the industry is a monopoly, then that one firm has a 100 percent share of the market, so that the HHI equals $(100)^2 = 10,000$.

1,800 as "moderately concentrated," and one with an HHI less than 1,000 as "unconcentrated." [98]   This convention will be followed in this study.[99]

Before turning to the HHI numbers, it is useful to examine the market shares of individual mutual fund complexes to see whether any single adviser firm or small group of firms accounts for a sizable portion of industry output.   Table 5.1 reports the market shares of the top 30 mutual fund complexes between 1982 and 1987.   These shares depend on the total number of mutual funds managed by an adviser as well as on the level of assets invested in each fund.   In the six-year interval from 1982 to 1987, the collective share of assets managed by the 30 largest complexes declined from 81.5 percent to 76.9 percent.   The declining market share of the largest complexes reflects the fact that smaller advisers as well as those new to the industry have been successful in gaining share at the expense of their larger rivals.

Table 5.2 presents the HHI values for mutual fund complexes, that is, for adviser firms.   In 1982, the HHI was 475.   By 1987, the index had fallen to 301.   Clearly, according to the Justice Department's guidelines, the mutual fund advisers compete in an unconcentrated market.   The low level of concentration in the mutual fund industry is evidence of the substantial degree of competition among mutual fund advisers.   Further, the downward trend in concentration indicates that competition in the mutual fund industry is increasing.

---

[98] Thus, see, e.g., W.J. Baumol, J.C. Panzar, and R.D. Willig, *Contestable Markets and the Theory of Industry Structures* (San Diego: Harcourt, Brace Jovanovich, revised edition, 1988).

[99] The HHI provides a useful measure of industry concentration because it is based upon information about all firms in the market. Other conventional measures, such as four- and eight-firm concentration ratios, in contrast, take into account only more limited information about the industry's leading firms.

Table 5.1

Thirty Largest Complexes' Percentage of Total Assets
1982-1987

Rank	1982	Share	1983	Share	1984	Share
1	Merrill Lynch Asset Mgmt. Inc.	14.2%	Merrill Lynch Asset Mgmt. Inc.	12.0%	Merrill Lynch Asset Mgmt. Inc.	10.8%
2	Dreyfus Corp.	8.3%	Federated Investors Corp.	7.9%	Federated Investors Corp.	6.8%
3	Federated Investors Corp.	8.0%	Dreyfus Corp.	7.0%	Dreyfus Corp.	6.2%
4	Fidelity Mgmt. & Research Co.	4.8%	Fidelity Mgmt. & Research Co.	5.2%	Fidelity Mgmt. & Research Co.	6.1%
5	Provident Inst'l Mgmt. Corp.	4.4%	Shearson/American Express	4.2%	Boston Company Advisors	4.5%
6	Shearson/American Express	4.4%	Provident Inst'l Mgmt. Corp.	3.7%	Kemper Financial Services Inc.	3.2%
7	Dean Witter Reynolds	3.6%	Kemper Financial Services Inc.	3.3%	IDS/American Express Inc.	2.6%
8	Kemper Financial Services Inc.	2.8%	Dean Witter Reynolds	2.9%	Dean Witter Reynolds	2.6%
9	E.F. Hutton	2.6%	IDS/American Express Inc.	2.6%	T. Rowe Price Associates	2.4%
10	Morgan Guaranty Trust	2.6%	T. Rowe Price Associates	2.5%	Vanguard Group	2.4%
11	Paine Webber	2.1%	E.F. Hutton	2.2%	Provident Inst'l Mgmt. Corp.	2.4%
12	T. Rowe Price Associates	2.1%	Capital Research & Mgmt. Co.	2.1%	E.F. Hutton	2.4%
13	IDS/American Express Inc.	2.1%	Vanguard Group	1.9%	Capital Research & Mgmt. Co.	2.3%
14	Oppenheimer Asset Mgmt. Corp.	2.1%	Morgan Guaranty Trust	1.8%	Oppenheimer Asset Mgmt. Corp.	2.2%
15	Capital Research & Mgmt. Co.	1.7%	Boston Company Advisors	1.8%	Wellington Mgmt. Co.	2.0%
16	Bache, Halsey, Stuart, Sheilds	1.5%	Paine Webber	1.5%	Shearson/American Express	1.8%
17	Vanguard Group	1.4%	Oppenheimer Asset Mgmt. Corp.	1.5%	Paine Webber	1.5%
18	Cont'l Ill. Nat'l Bank	1.4%	Goldman, Sachs & Co.	1.4%	Goldman, Sachs & Co.	1.5%
19	Wellington Mgmt. Co.	1.4%	Wellington Mgmt. Co.	1.4%	Putnam Mgmt. Co Inc.	1.5%
20	Goldman, Sachs & Co.	1.2%	Mass Financial Services Company	1.4%	Prudential Insurance Co.	1.4%

continued on next page

Table 5.1 continued

Rank	1982	Share	1983	Share	1984	Share
21	Mass Financial Services Co.	1.2%	Prudential-Bache Securities	1.4%	Mass Financial Services Co.	1.4%
22	Reserve Mgmt. Corp.	1.2%	Putnam Mgmt. Co. Inc.	1.2%	Franklin Distributor Inc.	1.4%
23	Benham Mgmt. Corp.	0.9%	American Capital Asset Mgmt. Inc.	1.0%	Prudential-Bache Securities	1.3%
24	Delaware Mgmt. Co.	0.9%	Cont'l Illinois National Bank	0.9%	American Capital Asset Mgmt.	1.2%
25	Putnam Mgmt. Co. Inc.	0.9%	Waddell & Reed Inc.	0.9%	Lord Abbett & Co.	0.9%
26	Oppenheimer Mgmt. Corp.	0.9%	Reserve Mgmt. Corp.	0.8%	Waddell & Reed Inc.	0.9%
27	Carnegie Capital Mgmt.	0.8%	Oppenheimer Mgmt. Corp.	0.8%	SEI Financial Services Co.	0.9%
28	Alliance Capital Mgmt. Corp.	0.8%	Lord Abbett & Co.	0.8%	Scudder Stevens & Clark	0.8%
29	Smith Barney	0.8%	Scudder Stevens & Clark	0.8%	Templeton Investment Counsel	0.8%
30	Lord Abbett & Co.	0.7%	Delaware Mgmt. Co.	0.8%	Pioneering Mgmt. Corp.	0.8%
Total		81.5%		77.8%		76.8%

continued on next page

Table 5.1 continued

Rank	1985	Share	1986	Share	1987	Share
1	Merrill Lynch Asset Mgmt. Inc.	10.2%	Merrill Lynch Asset Mgmt. Inc.	9.0%	Merrill Lynch Asset Mgmt. Inc.	8.2%
2	Federated Investors Corp.	6.1%	Fidelity Mgmt. & Research Co.	6.7%	Fidelity Mgmt. & Research Co.	7.1%
3	Fidelity Mgmt. & Research Co.	5.8%	Dreyfus Corp.	5.2%	Federated Investors Corp.	5.0%
4	Dreyfus Corp.	5.7%	Federated Investors Corp.	5.1%	Dreyfus Corp.	4.6%
5	Boston Company Advisors	4.7%	Boston Company Advisors	3.9%	Franklin Advisers Inc.	3.9%
6	Kemper Financial Services Inc.	3.2%	Dean Witter Reynolds	3.8%	Boston Company Advisors	3.8%
7	Dean Witter Reynolds	3.1%	Vanguard Group	3.3%	Dean Witter Reynolds	3.8%
8	E.F. Hutton	2.9%	Kemper Financial Services Inc.	3.2%	Vanguard Group	3.4%
9	Vanguard Group	2.8%	Franklin Advisers, Inc.	3.2%	Kemper Financial Services Inc.	3.2%
10	Provident Inst'l Mgmt. Corp.	2.5%	E.F. Hutton	2.4%	Putnam Mgmt. Co. Inc.	3.1%
11	IDS/American Express Inc.	2.3%	Prudential-Bache Securities	2.4%	Prudential-Bache Securities	2.6%
12	Wellington Mgmt. Co.	2.2%	Prudential Insurance Co.	2.4%	Prudential Insurance Co.	2.6%
13	T. Rowe Price Associates	2.1%	Wellington Mgmt. Co.	2.3%	E.F. Hutton	2.4%
14	Capital Research & Mgmt. Co.	2.0%	Putnam Mgmt. Co. Inc.	2.3%	Wellington Mgmt. Co.	2.3%
15	Shearson/American Express	2.0%	IDS/American Express Inc.	2.1%	Shearson Lehman Brothers Inc.	2.1%
16	Goldman, Sachs & Co.	1.9%	Provident Inst'l Mgmt. Corp.	2.0%	IDS/American Express Inc.	2.0%
17	Franklin Distributor Inc.	1.8%	Capital Research & Mgmt. Co.	2.0%	American Capital Asset Mgmt.	1.9%
18	Putnam Mgmt. Co. Inc.	1.6%	Shearson Lehman Brothers Inc.	1.9%	Capital Research & Mgmt. Co.	1.8%
19	Prudential-Bache Securities	1.6%	American Capital Asset Mgmt.	1.9%	Provident Inst'l Mgmt. Corp.	1.7%
20	Prudential Insurance Co.	1.5%	T. Rowe Price Associates	1.8%	Paine Webber	1.6%

continued on next page

Table 5.1 continued

Rank	1985	Share	1986	Share	1987	Share
21	Paine Webber	1.5%	Paine Webber	1.6%	T. Rowe Price Associates	1.6%
22	Mass Financial Services Co.	1.2%	Goldman, Sachs & Co.	1.4%	Goldman, Sachs & Co.	1.3%
23	Aim Management	1.1%	Mass Financial Services Co.	1.1%	Mass Financial Services Co.	1.2%
24	American Capital Asset Mgmt.	1.0%	Aim Management	1.0%	Scudder Stevens & Clark	1.1%
25	SEI Financial Services Co.	1.0%	Colonial Mgmt. Associates	1.0%	Colonial Mgmt. Associates	1.0%
26	Oppenheimer Asset Mgmt. Corp.	1.0%	Scudder Stevens & Clark	0.9%	Aim Advisors Inc.	0.8%
27	Colonial Mgmt. Associates	0.8%	Templeton Investment Counsel	0.8%	SEI Financial Mgmt. Corp.	0.8%
28	Templeton Investment Counsel	0.8%	Keystone Massachusetts Group	0.8%	Keystone Massachusetts Group	0.8%
29	Waddell & Reed Inc.	0.8%	SEI Financial Mgmt. Corp.	0.8%	Templeton Investment Counsel	0.8%
30	Scudder Stevens & Clark	0.8%	Oppenheimer Asset Mgmt. Corp.	0.8%	Alliance Capital Mgmt. Corp.	0.7%
Total		75.8%		77.0%		76.9%

Note: Data are as of 3/31, except for those of 1987, which are as of 12/31/86.
Source: Lipper — Directors' Analytical Data (1982-1987).

Table 5.2

Herfindahl-Hirschman Index for Mutual Fund Complexes
1982-1987

Year	1982	1983	1984	1985	1986	1987
HHI	475	393	350	327	307	301

Note: HHI calculated as of 3/31 for a given year, except for that of 1987, which is as of 12/31/86.

CONDITIONS OF ENTRY

The beneficial economic effects of competition are strengthened by unimpeded entry. Actual entry, or even the threat of entry, forces incumbent suppliers to be more efficient and responsive to consumer demand, while encouraging the pace of innovation and inducing firms to reduce prices and improve product performance. The presence of entry barriers impedes the optimal flow of resources into an industry[100] and may permit incumbent firms to charge prices that exceed competitive levels.

The strongest evidence of the ease of entry that characterizes the mutual fund industry is the remarkable amount of entry that has actually occurred both in the form of new funds and new advisory firms. After all, an industry that experiences a great deal of entry cannot be closed off by effective entry barriers. Nevertheless, despite the obvious weight of the entry statistics, we will also examine the various types of entry barriers recognized in the economics literature

---

[100] It is, however, possible to imagine conditions under which entry barriers may actually improve the allocation of resources from a welfare point of view. See C. C. von Weizsacker, "A Welfare Analysis of Barriers to Entry," *The Bell Journal of Economics*, vol. 11, no. 2 (Autumn, 1980), 399-420.

and provide evidence of their absence in the mutual fund industry.

A review of the record of entry of both funds and advisers suggests that significant entry barriers cannot be present in the mutual fund industry. Table 5.3 shows the net number of new mutual funds by year, for the period 1976-1987, in two categories: (1) equity, bond, and income funds, and (2) money market funds. From 1976 to 1987, the number of funds has increased at an average annual rate of 14.1 percent for the former and 27.2 percent for the latter.

Table 5.3 Net New Mutual Funds 1976-1987		
Year	Equity, bond, and income	Money market
1976	14	12
1977	23	2
1978	17	11
1979	2	15
1980	12	30
1981	28	73
1982	53	139
1983	114	55
1984	167	53
1985	251	34
1986	285	27
1987	425	56

Source: Investment Company Institute, *Mutual Fund Fact Book*, 1984-1988 editions.

Despite this record of persistent and substantial entry, one may question whether the record really demonstrates the absence of entry barriers in the industry if new funds have been created mainly by advisers of mutual funds already in existence. However, such doubts are readily dispelled by the facts. New mutual funds have been created both by existing mutual fund advisers and by advisers supplying mutual funds for the first time. As Figure 5.1 shows, the rate of entry into advisory activities has been considerable. For example, the net rate at which new advisers entered averaged 16.1 percent in 1983, 8.3 percent in 1987, and 12.7 percent over the entire period for which data are available. These statistics suggest that entry by new advisers of mutual funds occurs frequently, so there can be no substantial entry barriers into this activity.

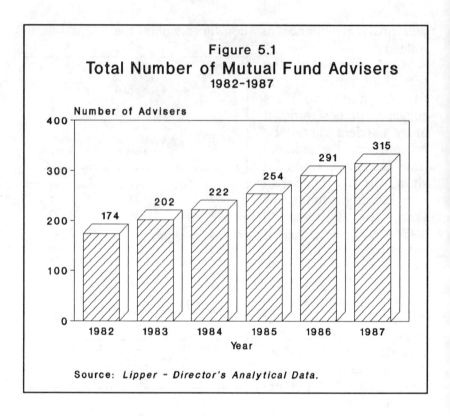

Figure 5.1
Total Number of Mutual Fund Advisers
1982-1987

Source: *Lipper - Director's Analytical Data.*

We can conclude with some confidence that the mutual fund industry is effectively free of entry barriers. The historical evidence indicates that entry into the market is not only feasible but easy. Under these conditions, advisers cannot hope to charge excessive fees for any sustained period. Excessive fees would only encourage new advisers to enter the market and lure customers away from the incumbents by charging lower but profitable fees to the advisory organization.

To reinforce our conclusion that no entry barriers exist in the mutual fund industry, we next review the direct evidence on the presence or absence of those entry barriers described in the economics literature. Those most commonly cited entry barriers are (1) the denial to entrants of production techniques or products available to incumbents and (2) the need to make capital investments in sunk assets in order to act as a producer in the industry. The absence of sunk investments means that an entrant, without any cost to itself, can withdraw any funds spent in the entry process should it decide to exit. Thus, by making entry riskless, the absence of sunk costs eliminates a basic impediment to the entry process. Either of these two barriers can conceivably restrict entry below the level most desirable for society, and the absence of both leads to a strong presumption that entry barriers are absent from an industry.

In the mutual fund industry, entrants have access to all of the technology available to firms already in operation. Neither specialized inputs nor proprietary production techniques characterize the production of mutual funds. Nor does government regulation confer any advantage on incumbent suppliers vis-a-vis entrants. Potential entrants have access to the same production technology that is used by incumbent funds. Thus, no such cost advantages to incumbents exist.

Economies of scale are sometimes interpreted as a barrier to entry.[101] When scale economies are present, a firm can produce efficiently only if the amount of product demanded from the firm is at least as great as the quantity that constitutes minimum efficient scale for the operations of the enterprise. Congress, the SEC, and others have argued that significant scale economies are generated by growth in the volume of assets under management in the mutual fund industry. In nearly every legal action questioning mutual fund advisory fees, the allegation has been made that the fee schedule established by the fund manager has failed to pass on to investors the cost savings derived from the fund's growing asset size. To determine whether economies of scale are present requires an extensive investigation of the underlying cost structure of mutual funds. Such an analysis will be reported in Chapter Seven.

---

[101] However, it is easy to demonstrate that scale economies do not prevent contestability, and consequently they are not in themselves a source of welfare losses. As a result, a number of analysts do not accept scale economies as an entry barrier.

INVESTOR MOBILITY

A third element governing the competitiveness of the mutual fund market is the magnitude of the transactions costs entailed when an investor switches from one fund to another. Investor mobility ensures that mutual fund advisers are in no position to expropriate the wealth of shareholders. In effect, low or zero cost to the individual investor entering a particular fund and/or exiting from that fund means that the investor faces little or no sunk costs from changing the investment. If sunk costs are low, there are no barriers to the association or disassociation of investor and firm.

Prior to the enactment of the 1940 Act, several features of the adviser-shareholder relationship caused the transactions costs of switching to be high and thus severely limited investor mobility. These features primarily stemmed from prohibitive restrictions that made it difficult for investors to redeem their shares. The impediments to investor mobility arose from (1) the prevailing closed-end form of the investment company, (2) the presence of front-end and back-end sales loads, exit, and entry charges, and (3) the illiquidity of the underlying assets of mutual funds.

Under the closed-end organizational form, which was predominant before 1940, investor mobility was inhibited by the fact that shares in such funds were not redeemed on demand. Further, in many cases, the shares were thinly traded so that the investor could not readily find an independent buyer for his shares. However, today most funds are mutual funds, or open-end investment companies, that redeem any or all of an investor's shares on demand on a given business day. Figure 5.2 illustrates the shift in popularity of closed-end funds relative to open-end funds. By 1987, the assets invested in closed-end funds had fallen to 2.6 percent of all investment company assets.

Large sales loads also limit investor mobility by increasing the transactions costs of switching. However, there has been a significant decline in sales loads in the industry. In 1966, almost 95 percent of total mutual fund assets were

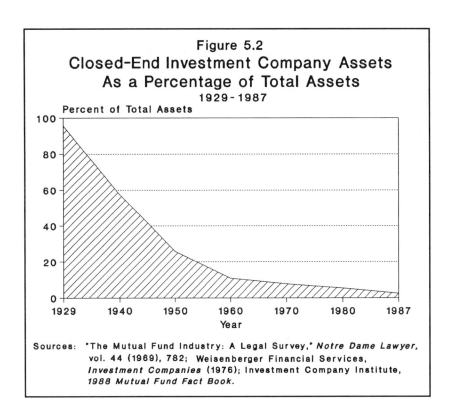

Figure 5.2
Closed-End Investment Company Assets
As a Percentage of Total Assets
1929-1987

Sources: "The Mutual Fund Industry: A Legal Survey," *Notre Dame Lawyer*, vol. 44 (1969), 782; Weisenberger Financial Services, *Investment Companies* (1976); Investment Company Institute, *1988 Mutual Fund Fact Book*.

invested in load funds, with typical sales loads ranging from 7.5 percent to 8.7 percent. By 1987, sales loads charged on low-load funds were as low as .95 percent; moreover, an increasing number of no-load funds had become available. Recently, sales of no-load funds have remained fairly constant, ranging from about 70 percent to 80 percent of total industry sales over the time period 1977 to 1987. In addition, back-end sales loads are now usually immaterial in magnitude, and a significant majority of funds do not have redemption fees at all. Of the small number of funds that do have redemption fees, the fees ranged from 0.25 percent to 6.0 percent in 1987.[102] The reduction in

---

[102] Donoghue Organization, Inc., *Donoghue's Mutual Funds Almanac*, 19th edition.

the transactions costs of switching attributable to diminished use of sales loads increases investor mobility and thus facilitates switching funds in reaction to excessive advisory fees.

Finally, the liquidity of the underlying assets of mutual funds has increased. For example, many funds provide automatic withdrawal privileges, a feature that expedites redemption. Many short-term mutual funds, such as MMFs, also offer check-writing privileges. Check writing simplifies redemption to the point where a check can be written at any time and can then serve as a medium of exchange. Typically, these funds require a minimum check size of $500.[103]

Several other mechanisms that promote fund liquidity have evolved in the mutual fund industry. For example, the recent development of mutual fund complexes has facilitated the offering of exchange privileges within a complex. As a result, investors can quickly move holdings from one fund to another at a reduced fee or with no fee at all. These exchanges can often be executed over the telephone. Shareholders have begun to take advantage of exchange privileges in reacting to changing market conditions. Figure 5.3 shows the rate of sales exchanges across all mutual funds between 1979 and 1987. In 1979, total sales exchanges were $5.8 billion relative to an industry asset base of $94.2 billion, for a rate of 6.2 percent in that year. By 1987, sales exchanges had increased to $205.7 billion relative to the asset base of $769.9 billion. This level of switching translates into a sales exchange rate of 26.7 percent for the year.

Similarly, wire transfer of investors' funds also increases the mobility available to shareholders. This service goes beyond the transfer of an investment among funds within a complex. For example, wire transfers allow investors to redeem shares in a fund instantaneously and transfer the money to a bank account.

These developments have markedly decreased the transactions costs of switching and increased investor mobility since the enactment of the 1940 Act. The high degree of investor

---

[103] *1988 Mutual Fund Fact Book.*

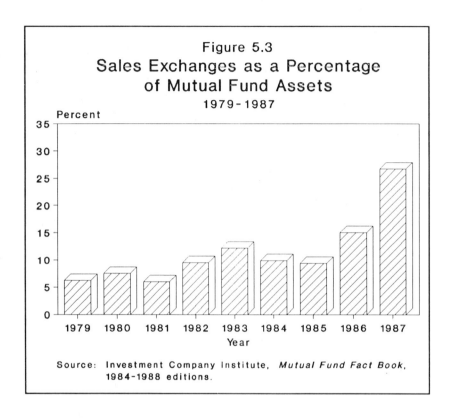

Figure 5.3
Sales Exchanges as a Percentage
of Mutual Fund Assets
1979-1987

Source: Investment Company Institute, *Mutual Fund Fact Book*, 1984-1988 editions.

mobility enhances the effectiveness of competition as a market governance mechanism. The possibility of abuses by advisers, which was the motivation for regulation, was created by investor immobility and the limited competitiveness of the industry at that time.

OUTLAYS ON INPUTS USED TO MAKE FINAL PRODUCTS SOLD ON COMPETITIVE MARKETS

The last of the pertinent structure-performance issues that is basic for our analysis involves the relationship between two firms, one of which sells final consumer products in a highly competitive market, while the other supplies inputs to it.

Such vertical relationships are usually judged to be less troubling from the viewpoint of the public welfare than is any direct association among horizontal competitors (that is, a relation between firms that sell similar products and those that compete for the same customers). If the horizontal competitors were to agree on prices or the quality of their products, customer welfare would obviously be threatened. There is no clear counterpart to this danger that stems from an agreement between a firm that sells inputs and one that buys them — indeed, it is well known that such an agreement can yield reduced prices to consumers as each of the firms undertakes to hold back on its share of the final product price, hoping to elicit an increase in sales volume that must benefit them both. That is, here *absence* of coordination causes an externalities problem that will harm consumers as well as both of the firms in question.

Still, relationships among vertically associated firms are often considered to give rise to two interrelated problems, one of which has generally been at the heart of the complaints that have been lodged in the courts against mutual fund advisory firms.

First, it is asserted that an input-buying firm that has some sort of bond with its input supplier will tend not to select the products of the most efficient supplier, but will either favor its associate or even be given no choice in the matter. Thus, when the CSX railroads proposed to merge with American Commercial Barge Lines, other barge operators objected, asserting that in the future, when CSX needed some barge services (as it often does), it would tend to purchase them from its own subsidiary, even if competing barge lines offered better service or lower prices. (The I.C.C. rejected this claim and permitted the merger.)

Second, it is feared that association of two firms, one of which buys inputs from the other, invites overpricing of the input, with the cost passed on to the consumers of the final product.

We will see, next, on what grounds economic analysis concludes that neither of these fears has any foundation if the market for the final product is sufficiently competitive. Indeed, *even if that market is not highly competitive*, but competition prevails in the input-supply market, the basis for these fears often turns out to be questionable. Let us see why this is so, taking the two (not unrelated) concerns in turn.

1. *The fear that an inefficient supplier will be favored.* At first, it seems plausible that, given a choice among suppliers of any input, the purchaser will prefer to buy from an inefficient affiliated supplier rather than from one that is (slightly) more efficient but unaffiliated. However, if *either* industry, that of input supply or that which uses the input to make the final product, is highly competitive, this fear makes no sense for a profit-maximizing input buyer.

   a. Where the final-product market is highly competitive, the reason is obvious. Thus, suppose the firm F, the producer of the final product in question, gets its input from a supplier A, whose costs are $50 per unit, but there are other input suppliers whose superior efficiency entails a cost of only $40 per unit. Then, if firm F buys from A, F's competitors and the more efficient input suppliers can, either by joining forces or simply by recourse to the market, make a profit selling the final product at a price lower than the price at which F can cover its costs. That is, F will then be faced with two equally suicidal choices: either to lose its customers to the products of its rivals, with their more attractive prices, or alternatively, to match its competitors' prices and make a loss on the sales of its product, a permanent drain on its finances. Clearly, then, firm F's only viable option, when the final-product market is so highly competitive, is to give up its purchases from its inefficient affiliate. But even if irrationality or some means of compulsion stop it from doing so, it does not matter to society. For such an intransigent firm F will soon be driven out of business, leaving the field to those rivals who make their purchases from efficient input suppliers only.

It is clear, then, on what basis economic analysis concludes that strong competitive forces in the final-product market preclude purchases of inputs from inefficient suppliers, no matter how strong the affiliation ties may be between the purchaser and the supplier.

b. Where the *input* market is highly competitive, a profit-maximizing producer of the final product will still avoid purchasing from an inefficient affiliate, even if the final product is *not* competitive. Here the reason is only a bit more subtle than that in the previous case. Now, the point is that every input purchase from an inefficient supplier inevitably entails a commensurate profit sacrifice for the final-product supplier, F. An example will make the point. Suppose that the profit-maximizing price for F's product is $200 and that at a $40 price of the input (one unit of which is used for each unit of final product) the (marginal) profit yield of the product is $30. Suppose, also, that an unaffiliated input supplier U can afford to supply the input at $40 per unit, but that the less efficient input supplier affiliate A incurs a marginal cost (or a per-unit incremental cost) of $50 in making the input.

Then, by the hypothesis that the input market is competitive, U will be forced to offer its input at a price of $40 (or something close to it). But affiliate A clearly cannot afford to offer that product at that price, and a price for the input that covers A's marginal cost and hence equals at least $50 must clearly cut F's marginal profit from $30 to $20 or less.

The same must be true even if A is a subsidiary of F and their costs and profits are merged. Then the choice of input supplier becomes a make-or-buy decision for firm F. If it chooses to buy the input, competition on the input market guarantees that its input cost will be close to $40. But if it decides to *make* the product it will instead incur a marginal (incremental) cost of $50 per unit, and the profit consequences will clearly be the same as before.

Incidentally, it was presumably the competitive-input market analysis that led to the I.C.C.'s approval of the merger between CSX railroads and American Commercial Barge Lines. Everyone agrees that at least some parts of the traffic transported by railroads are not carried under highly competitive conditions. But few would question that barge transportation is sold in a highly competitive (contestable) market.

We can now deal succinctly with the second concern about affiliation between the supplier and the purchaser of an input (the concern that is the more pertinent one for money-market advisory services).

2. *The fear that an input purchaser will permit an affiliated input supplier to overprice its product, passing the excess on to consumers of the final product.* A moment's consideration should confirm that *exactly* the same forces that preclude purchases from inefficient input suppliers also prevent the overpricing of the input, if *either* the final-product market or the input market is highly competitive. An excessive input price causes exactly the same problems for the seller of the final goods as are caused by the high costs of an inefficient input supplier. If the final-product market is competitive, purchases of an overpriced input must drive the final-product producer out of the market, either because it will be out-performed by rivals who buy their inputs at a lower price, or because of losses incurred as it tries to absorb the excessive input price. Even if the final-product market is not competitive, competition in the input market means that purchase of the overpriced input offered by an affiliate must entail a profit sacrifice.[104]

---

[104] In this case, however, when the affiliates are both subsidiaries of the same enterprise, the *excessive price* of the input will have no economic

It should be noted that none of the impediments to over-pricing of inputs that have just been described is not to be attributed in any way to resistance or unwillingness by one of the parties, or the inability of the other party to enforce its wishes. Even if both parties wish to join in the overpricing game and cooperate fully with one another, competitive market forces simply will not allow them to do so.

A final example should nail down the point. Imagine a barge line that purchases its fuel from its proprietor's brother-in-law. Even if the barge line owner would find life intolerable at home if he were to switch to another fuel supplier, it is obvious that there is no way in which the brother-in-law could enforce a fuel price significantly above the market level, for that would reduce the competitiveness of the barge line, and soon enough make it vulnerable to the incursions of rivals. The point is that tightness of affiliation between input seller and input buyer makes no difference to the power of market forces to preclude overpricing of an input.

In all this, it is somewhat ironic that concern is much more often expressed about vertical transactions between two different (if affiliated) firms than about similar transactions that occur entirely within the same firm, with one of its divisions supplying an input to another. One never hears of claims that transactions of that sort entail abusive coordinated action of the entities involved, even though in such cases the power to enforce such coordination is apt to be at its maximum. It is, curiously, only where the buyer and seller of the input are *different* firms that concerns such as overpricing of inputs or inefficient input supply surface regularly.

---

significance if the final-product price is unaffected. If the final-product seller is a profit-maximizing monopoly, that final-product price — the profit-maximizing price — will indeed be unaffected by a rise of the bookkeeping-transfer price of the input. For that price rise will do no more than redistribute the accountants' division of the firm's total profits between the share attributed to the firm's input production activities and that assigned to its final-product manufacture.

INDUSTRY CONDUCT UNDER PERFECT COMPETITION AND CONTESTABILITY

The two market forms that have just been discussed prove far less reliable as guarantors of good business conduct than they are of good performance, as judged by the conventional criteria. The literature provides an analysis of the circumstances under which firms will find it profitable to misrepresent or to adulterate their products.[105] It concludes, as should hardly be surprising, that a market populated by fly-by-night firms is most likely to generate such problems, while in an industry made up of a few firms that are all well known, with few newcomers and few enterprises exiting, reputation becomes a valuable asset, and firms will be disinclined to risk it for the earnings that can be contributed by misleading of customers and surreptitious reduction of product quality.

Where firms enter and exit quickly and easily, some of them are likely to be relatively unknown to the buying public generally. But a relatively anonymous seller who does not expect to be recognized or remembered is concomitantly in a position to gain from false claims, withholding of information, and shoddy products. More than that, the more common such practices are in a particular market, the more likely it is that firms that want very much to conduct themselves well will find it difficult not to join in the process of competition in degradation of both their products and the information provided by them to consumers. For if unhappy experiences associated with purchases in the past lead consumers to have little faith in the norms of conduct in the industry, then even the holdouts will find themselves under suspicion, and will gain little from their attempt to preserve their integrity.

The point in all this is that the very ease of exit and entry that makes for good performance in perfectly competitive

---

[105] The contribution to the subject that is, perhaps, most frequently cited is that of Carl Shapiro. See Carl Shapiro, "Consumer Information, Product Quality, and Seller Reputation," *The Bell Journal of Economics*, vol. 13, no. 1 (Spring, 1982), 20-35.

and perfectly contestable markets also makes it likely that there will be some entrants with little reputation; and if some among these also care little about good conduct, conditions are apt to deteriorate. Ease of exit, as measured by a low share of sunk cost, can exacerbate the problem, because it means that the risk to the firm entailed by bad business conduct in such an arena is minimal. If the firm is caught out, it need merely exit, taking its (unsunk) investments along.

In such cases, then, consumers are likely to need some sort of protection to prevent them from falling victim to misleading information or adulterated products.

CONCLUSIONS

The preceding pages can be interpreted as a summary of the portions of industrial-organization analysis that are most pertinent to the issues about the relationship between money market mutual funds and their advisers. The discussion quickly reviewed the very familiar doctrines on the role of competition in ensuring good performance in terms of economic efficiency and preclusion of excessive prices and profits. However, it was pointed out that the issues of monopoly or oligopoly that are the focus of this standard discussion are not the pertinent matters for the industry with which this book concerns itself. Rather, the critical issues concern the vertical relations between input suppliers (the suppliers of advisory services) and the purchasers of those inputs, along with what is probably a subsidiary issue, namely the incentives for keeping money market fund investors inadequately informed, and other related varieties of supplier misconduct.

Even if it is less widely known, the literature of industrialization offers well-developed analyses of these issues, and it is this material that constituted the bulk of the preceding recapitulation of the pertinent analysis. That discussion provided grounds for the conclusion that there is little to be feared from the vertical relationship between the funds and their advisers, though such a conclusion can hardly be accepted with complete confidence until the institutional circumstances and the available quantitative evidence have been analyzed in detail. It is to these matters that the remainder of this book addresses itself.

SIX

THE DEMAND FOR MONEY MARKET MUTUAL FUNDS

As discussed in previous chapters, the Investment Company Act was designed to protect investors from financial abuse of their interests by advisers of mutual funds. One important dimension of the perceived need for such regulation was the determination of the fees charged by mutual fund advisers. It has been suggested that advisers are in the enviable position of being able to set fees that are excessively high with little or no risk of driving their customers away. Underlying this view is the perception that the nature of the contract between the investment adviser and the mutual fund denies investors the opportunity to replace the adviser if his behavior is unacceptable. This view assumes implicitly that mutual fund shareholders are either unable or unlikely to discipline the adviser by shopping around for the most attractive place to invest their money.

Economists, of course, are naturally suspicious of arguments based on the premise that government intervention is called for because individuals are not sufficiently astute to protect their own interests, although there do exist circumstances in which such concerns are well founded. In the arena under discussion, economists generally proceed on the presumption that individuals select mutual funds, among other considerations, on the basis of the relative expected rates of return offered by the various funds. When this presumption is consistent with the facts, all else being equal, individual advisers who attempt to exercise market power by raising and maintaining fees above competitive levels face the very real prospect that market forces will penalize their conduct, since higher fees necessarily lead to a lower net yield.

This view of market discipline was eloquently expressed by Judge Pollock in the First District Court case, *Gartenberg v. Merrill Lynch*, when he noted

> Money market shareholders hold the key to the continuance of the adviser in charge of their funds. They can terminate the relationship simply by writing a check and redeeming at once. This is the strongest kind of bargaining power against compensation that is improper.

As we have seen, among courts, this view is distinctly in the minority. More typically, economic arguments of this sort have either been ignored or dismissed. For example, as noted, the Appellate Court in *Gartenberg v. Merrill Lynch* opined that advisers' fees are relatively small for each shareholder and therefore "do not figure significantly in the battle for investor favor."

This divergence of opinion amounts to an empirical dispute about the degree of shareholder sensitivity to the level of net yield offered by a mutual fund. Thus, rational resolution of the dispute requires recourse to empirical evidence, and that evidence is what this chapter undertakes to provide. We begin with a general discussion of measures of the sensitivity (elasticity) of customer demand to variations in the financial terms on which a good or service is offered, and then report the results of a statistical study of shareholder demand for MMFs. The central point of the study is to determine whether or not investors' demands are sufficiently sensitive to small differences in the yields of different funds to constitute a substantial business threat to those advisers who overcharge for their services. We restrict our attention to MMFs, since this area, exclusively, has been the battleground for disputes over advisory fees since the amendments to the ICA were adopted in 1970.

DEMAND ELASTICITY: AN INTRODUCTION

As just noted, the key empirical issue here is the responsiveness of investor demand for MMFs to variations in the net yields offered by these funds. The measure conventionally used to evaluate this responsiveness is the elasticity of the demand function, which can be defined as the percent reduction in demand for a product that results from a one percent increase in its price.[106] To apply this concept to the present analysis, the pertinent "price" must be recognized to be the net yield of a fund, or the fund's gross yield less its expense ratio. When consumers are quite responsive to a price change, we say that demand is highly elastic, with a value of unity being the dividing line between elastic and inelastic demand.[107]

The concept of demand elasticity can be applied to both the market demand facing the aggregate of firms in an industry and to the demand facing individual firms. The market demand elasticity is determined primarily by the availability of substitutes, while the elasticity facing individual firms is a function of the availability of these substitutes and the number of other firms that supply identical products. Market demand for a good or service may be highly inelastic if consumers have no viable substitutes for that product so that they have no place to turn if the current supplier raises price (reduces yields) substantially. However, if many firms supply the same product, the market demand may be highly inelastic, even though individual firms face a highly elastic demand.

The concept of demand elasticity bears a critical relation to the concept of market power, by which we mean the ability

---

[106] If the demand function for x as a function of price is denoted by $x(p)$, then elasticity is defined mathematically by the following derivative: (dx/dp) $x(p/x)$.

[107] A demand elasticity is negative in value because price increases are associated with reductions in quantity demanded. In contrast, since an increase in its relative net yield, or "price," will increase the demand facing a fund, the values of the demand elasticity in the present context are normally positive.

of a firm or a coalition of firms to raise prices above competitive levels and maintain them for a substantial period of time. In competitive markets, no single firm acting independently of the others is in a position to raise and maintain price above competitive levels. In such a case, market power is denied to individual firms in the industry. In general, the degree to which an individual firm is in a position to exercise market power is inversely related to the elasticity of the demand for its product, since, by definition, when a firm's demand elasticity is high, any attempt by it to impose a high price will elicit a substantial drop in its volume of business.

Demand elasticity can be evaluated in a number of ways. It can be assessed qualitatively by considering such influences as the availability of substitutes, availability of information, and investor mobility. Or it can be measured econometrically by statistical regression techniques. Either approach can be used to study the market as a whole or the circumstances facing the individual firm. We begin our assessment of demand elasticity with an examination of the characteristics of the MMF industry overall and the availability of substitute instruments. We then use statistical regression techniques to estimate a market share model from which it is possible to derive estimates of the degree of demand elasticity facing individual funds in the industry.

ELASTICITY OF MARKET DEMAND FOR MONEY MARKET MUTUAL FUNDS

The degree of market demand elasticity in an industry is determined primarily by the ease of availability of substitute products. When consumers have ready access to alternatives, they cannot be exploited by a firm or group of firms attempting to raise prices above competitive levels. Money market mutual funds compete with a wide array of financial instruments. At any point, their relative attractiveness is determined by investors who continuously evaluate the differentials in risk-adjusted rates of return among different financial instruments.

A number of these financial products offer risk-adjusted yields comparable to those provided by MMFs, and they must, therefore, be considered substitute products.

Advisers of MMFs serve as financial intermediaries who make available to consumers a portfolio of short-term money market assets. However, investment in money market assets can be carried out through a variety of alternative channels. Individual consumers may invest directly in the underlying assets that compose mutual money market fund portfolios. While many small investors cannot meet the minimum investment requirements for some of these assets, what matters is that there are enough investors at the margin who are not constrained by the amount of wealth required to meet minimum investment rules. Shareholders of money market funds also have the alternative of placing their funds in various types of deposit accounts offered by banks and thrift institutions. Currently, such alternatives include NOW accounts and MMDAs. Of course, these instruments date from the 1980s, and it is quite possible that their introduction served to increase the elasticity of demand for MMFs in the aggregate.[108] In sum, alternative short-term money market investment opportunities are available to consumers through either direct investment or commercial banks and thrift institutions. Mutual funds comprise only one medium for investment in these assets.

In addition to money market instruments, a wide variety of other assets exist that serve as substitutes for MMFs. Relevant substitute assets include equities or fixed income securities, whether acquired directly by investors or through investment in mutual funds. Such assets, of course, have very

---

[108] See Sherman Maisel and Kenneth Rosen, *Macroeconomics of Money Market Mutual Funds*, Working Paper 82-56, Center for Real Estate and Urban Economics, University of California, Berkeley (December 1982). The authors have investigated the influence of money market funds on consumer interest rate elasticities, maturity preferences, and sensitivity to risk. The econometric results obtained confirm that investors react to rate differentials among financial assets. Their results also suggest that the introduction of MMDAs caused an increase in the degree of sensitivity to interest rate differentials.

different characteristics from money market funds, particularly in terms of risk. Nonetheless, in theory at least, equilibrium in the capital market requires all assets to earn approximately equivalent risk-adjusted rates of return.[109] In the event that advisers of MMFs collectively were to undertake a non-competitive fee increase, thus reducing the risk-adjusted yields of the funds, investors in money market funds would be likely to divert their assets into other securities, thereby exerting enough market pressure to re-equilibriate the yields on money market and other capital market assets.

Another determinant of the competitiveness of a market is the cost of information. Investors in MMFs can quickly obtain information on these funds as well as on competing financial assets. Several mail letters and almanacs provide complete coverage of the performance of mutual funds, and of MMFs in particular. Shareholders can obtain yield quotes directly by either calling the money market fund or turning to the financial pages of newspapers. Consequently, shareholders can constantly be in a position to make informed investment decisions at little cost.

A third determinant of the competitiveness of a market is the ease with which consumers can switch their product purchases. If a consumer must incur costs when changing suppliers, his incentive to switch in response to an increase in relative price is reduced. Stated differently, the expected gain from switching must be equal to or greater than the cost of switching — the higher the cost, the greater the required expected gain necessary to elicit a transfer of funds.

In fact, actual and potential investors can easily enter MMFs and switch their capital into new investments. The majority of noninstitutional MMFs require only a modest minimum investment, and even lower minimums are imposed for incremental investments. Redemption is just as easy, and MMFs have no up-front or back-end sales load, both of which

---

[109] For a discussion, see Eugene Fama and Merton Miller, *The Theory of Finance* (New York: Holt, Rinehart, and Winston, 1972), and Fama, *Foundations of Finance* (New York: Basic Books, 1976).

directly increase transactions costs. Most money market funds facilitate redemptions by allowing investors to write drafts against their shares at no charge. In addition, since interest is taxed as earned, regardless of when the shares are actually redeemed, there are no detrimental tax consequences associated with redemption. Consequently, since transaction costs are so low, the prospect of only modest gains can induce investors to switch their capital into higher-yielding assets.

All of these conditions encourage investors to react relatively quickly in response to variations in the fees charged by fund advisers. Under such conditions, one would expect industry demand to be highly elastic and behavior by suppliers to be competitive. With the availability of comparable alternatives and the opportunity to monitor performance statistics easily, investors in MMFs would seem to be unlikely targets for abuse by money market fund advisers.

FUND ELASTICITY OF DEMAND

Although we have not yet provided any empirical measures of the elasticity of demand in the MMF industry, we have shown that the industry is characterized by attributes known to be associated with a high elasticity of demand. Moreover, because many money market funds offer highly substitutable alternatives, the demand facing an individual fund is even more elastic than the demand for the market as a whole.[110] When demand is highly elastic, no single MMF has the ability to profit from noncompetitive behavior.

The next section attempts to measure the demand elasticity facing an individual fund by relating a fund's market share to that fund's relative net yield among other variables.

---

[110] For a discussion of the relative elasticity of industry and individual firm demand, see William M. Landes and Richard A. Posner, "Market Power in Antitrust Cases," *Harvard Law Review*, vol. 94, no. 5 (1981), 937-996; and Ordover, Sykes, and Willig, "Herfindahl Concentration, Rivalry, and Mergers," *Harvard Law Review*, vol. 95, no. 8 (1982), 1857-1874.

In this way, we can directly test the null hypothesis that shareholders in MMFs are not sensitive to the fees charged by their respective advisers. Since net yield is equal to gross yield less total fees charged to shareholders, a corollary to the finding that investors respond to the relative net yields of different funds is that shareholders also react to total fees through the direct effect of fees on net yield. Given a measure of net yield elasticity, it is also possible to estimate the fund demand elasticity with respect to total fees. Such estimates will be reported later in this chapter.

Theoretical Specification of the Model

The primary objective of the model of the market shares of MMFs is to measure the degree of investor sensitivity to net yield differentials among funds. The model assumes that at time t the total demand for MMFs is known and is given by the sum of the amounts to be invested by different individuals in MMFs.[111] For any single MMF, the quantity of assets invested in that fund at time t is a function of (1) the expected net yield or rate of return on investment in the fund, (2) the expected return on competing funds, (3) a vector of quality and service attributes, and (4) the total number of funds among which the investors can select. Thus, at time t the portion of MMF assets managed by fund i is

$$m_{it} = f(r_{1t}, ..., r_{it}, ..., r_{nt}, a_{it}, n_t)$$ (6.1)

where

m_{it} = the market share of assets held by fund i at time t;

---

[111] Standard portfolio selection theory describes how investors determine the proportion of wealth to be allocated to each asset type. For more on this subject, see Fama, *Foundations of Finance,* op. cit. The use of the market share as the unit of analysis is also quite standard.

r_{it} = the expected rate of return on fund i at time t;
a_{it} = a vector of quality and service attributes of
     fund i at time t;
n_t = the total number of available funds at time t.

Theory predicts that the share of assets invested in MMF i will increase when the fund's own expected rate of return increases. Theory also predicts that the share of assets invested in fund i will decrease when the expected rate of return on competing MMFs increases. That is, the assets consumers invest in a particular fund depend on the return that the fund offers in comparison with the return the investor could earn in alternative funds. We can get some approximate sense of this relationship by examining Figure 6.1, which relates a fund's yield index— i.e., the net yield of a fund relative to the average net yield of all funds — to the fund's market share. For the years 1980 to 1987, the figure shows the yield index for each of three groups of funds. The higher the net yield provided by a group of funds, the more successful the group has been in attracting shareholder assets. While this is qualitatively the sort

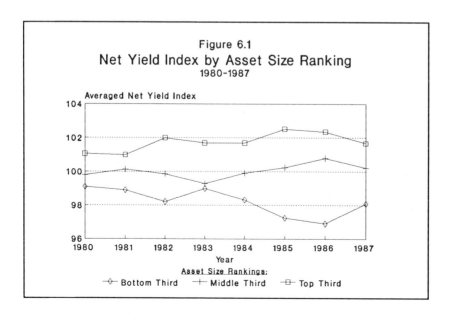

Figure 6.1
Net Yield Index by Asset Size Ranking
1980-1987

of result one would expect *a priori*, the purpose of our empirical study of fund demand is to quantify and test this relationship more formally.

Whereas standard portfolio theory explicitly takes into account risk differences among the different securities, our model only considers rates of return and assumes that risk is the same for all MMFs. Money market mutual funds also offer shareholders a variety of nonrate features. For any two funds with identical expected rates of return, our model implies that the fund with higher quality and service standards will manage a larger portion of the total assets invested in MMF portfolios. All else equal, funds that provide relatively extensive services will charge higher total fees. In selecting among different funds, investors weigh the value of the additional services against the reduction in net yield caused by higher fees. Consequently, the existence of lower-yielding funds with relatively greater market shares can be explained by differences in the services offered. Finally, one would expect that the percent of assets managed by any single fund is inversely related to the total number of available funds. If all funds offered identical net yields and were of equal quality, the expected market share of any single fund would be $1/n$, where n is the number of available mutual money market funds.

A Workable Econometric Model

To move from the general form of equation (6.1) above to a formulation that is usable for empirical work requires a number of additional steps, including a more precise specification of the relevant variables and a choice of functional form. The first issue concerns the manner in which the net yield variable is to be introduced. Obviously, because of the large number of MMFs, it is not possible to take into account all the individual rates of return encompassed in equation (6.1), so some simplification is necessary. A common simplification, which we adopt, is to use the ratio of a fund's net yield to the average net yield paid by all funds.[112] In our empirical demand model, we employ the variable YDIN to measure the relative rate of return on the assets of a given fund, which is defined as the ratio of the net yield of fund *i* over period *t* to the average net yield of all funds over period *t*. The time unit used in our study is a year.[113]

In addition to determining the nature of the relative net yield variable, it is also necessary to select variables to represent the service and quality features of a fund and the number of alternative MMFs available to investors. Because of unavailability of some data, we employ variables that serve as proxies for the true variables whose effects the model is intended to measure. The variables experimented with in the demand model are the following:

FUNDS_{it} = total number of mutual funds managed by the adviser of fund *i* in year *t*

BROKER_i = 1 if shares in fund *i* may be bought through stockbrokers affiliated with the fund's distributors; 0 otherwise

AGEIN_{it} = the age of fund *i* in year *t* divided by the average age of all funds in year *t*

ALLDOM_t = total number of retail, taxable nongovernment funds in year *t*

---

[112]This procedure was used successfully by S. M. Goldfeld, "Savings and Loan Associations and the Market for Savings," *A Study of the Savings and Loan Industry*, vol. 2, I. Friend, ed., Federal Home Loan Bank Board (1969), 569-658. We should also note that we are using actual net yields as a proxy for expected returns.

[113]Net yield as used in the demand model corresponds to the total return per share over year *t*. Since MMFs maintain a constant net asset value, the realized return stems exclusively from income earned by the money market assets in the fund's portfolio. For purposes of our modeling effort, we have estimated a fund's market share on the basis of end-of-year assets.

Data on net yield, assets, and broker funds were obtained from *Donoghue's Mutual Fund Almanac* and *Donoghue's Money Fund Report*. Data on the FUNDS variable were obtained from *Lipper — Directors' Analytical Data*.

The total number of mutual funds managed by the adviser of the money market fund is used as one proxy for service levels. Money market mutual funds are typically part of a larger complex of mutual funds. Many funds allow shareholders to transfer assets from one mutual fund to another without incurring costly transaction charges. The ability to do this means that investors can quickly respond to net yield differentials among different types of mutual funds. A second feature of the larger fund complexes is that they often embody more comprehensive communications networks than smaller fund complexes. For the investor, this may mean that a fund that is part of a larger complex can provide more efficient service. For these reasons, we would expect increased values of the FUNDS variable to have a positive influence on market share. One would also expect the coefficient of FUNDS to be positive if economies of scale or scope are associated with increased size of complexes.

By having a broker/dealer affiliate, a fund is likely to be able to facilitate security transactions of its shareholders requiring a broker intermediary, so that it should also serve to increase market share. That is, the coefficient of the affiliate variable can also be expected to be positive. Another demand-stimulating effect that the BROKER variable may capture is the effectiveness of different channels of distribution of fund assets. Since distributing shares through broker affiliates may be more or less effective than direct distribution, this effect could either be positive or negative. Thus, should the sign on the BROKER coefficient be positive, it will not be possible to distinguish the distribution from the service component. If the sign is negative, however, this would suggest that despite the possible service benefits, the distribution of shares through broker affiliates is less effective than direct distribution.

Since the shareholders of MMFs are not protected by deposit insurance, a fund's market share may be affected by the riskiness or stability it is perceived to possess. To the extent that investors have greater confidence in older funds that have a proven track record, a reasonable proxy for this perceived risk effect is the relative age of a fund, with the presumption that, all else equal, older funds enjoy a larger market share. In addition, older funds may have a first-mover advantage in the sense that once shareholders have invested in a fund, as long as the fund continues to provide a competitive net yield, shareholders have a reduced incentive to invest either their current assets or additional assets in a different fund. In turn, this implies that the relative age of a fund is apt to be related positively to market share. The final variable ALLDOM is the number of alternative MMFs available to investors. We have already discussed why this variable should be inversely related to the expected market share of a given fund.

Econometric Results

The statistical analysis was based on a sample of all retail, taxable money market funds having similar investment objectives, using data for the period 1980 to 1986. Those funds that restrict their investments exclusively to government issues were excluded from the sample, since the risk associated with these funds was judged to differ systematically from the risk of the other funds included in our sample.[114]
Summary statistics by year for the data used in our sample are given in Table 6.1. Confirming the general growth of the industry discussed in earlier chapters, the table shows steady growth in the total number of funds over time. Over the same period, the average net yield has displayed substantial

---

[114] Simple hypothesis testing of the equality of means and variances among different groups of MMFs having different investment objectives revealed that government funds differ statistically from other groups of funds we analyzed. Similar tests did not allow us to reject the hypothesis that the means and variance of nongovernment funds were equal. Four groups of non-government funds were tested. They were termed (1) Domestic Prime; (2) Domestic Prime Euro; (3) Domestic Prime Euro-Yankee; and (4) Aggressive.

fluctuation. The average age of funds fell in 1982 to 3.6 years because of the large number of new funds, but has since increased to 6.1 years in 1986. The percentage of funds that distribute shares through a broker/dealer affiliate declined from 35.8 percent in 1980 to 20.5 percent in 1986, reflecting the fact that many of the newer funds are general-purpose funds that distribute their shares directly to investors. The sample comprised 754 firms from 1980 through 1986.[115]

Equation (6.2) below is the functional form that was utilized in our analysis. The function is linear in the logarithm of the variables, with the exception of the BROKER variable, which simply assumes the value of either 0 or 1. Thus, estimated in equation form:

$$\ln m_{it} = b_0 + b_1 \ln YDIN + b_2 \ln FUNDS + b_3 \ln ALLDOM + b_4 \ln AGEIN + b_5 BROKER \qquad (6.2)$$

We experimented with the equation by introducing ALLDOM and FUNDS in linear fashion. We also tried introducing the relative age variable, AGEIN, both by itself and as a cross-product with the logarithm of YDIN. The results obtained by estimating the parameters of these various forms by ordinary least squares are reported in Table 6.2. Although we do not report the details, we also examined the structural stability over time of the estimates of the various equation forms by a series of Chow tests, and no evidence of instability emerged. This permits us to interpret the results in a relatively straightforward fashion.

---

[115] Note that the number of firms in our sample is slightly lower than the total number of funds as a result of cases with missing data.

Table 6.1

Summary Statistics for Data Used in Market Share Regression, All Retail Taxable Nongovernment Funds
1980-1986

	1980	1981	1982	1983	1984	1985	1986
Total number of observations	53	68	97	121	134	138	143
Average net yield (%)	12.12	17.10	12.50	8.66	10.14	7.71	6.26
	(0.36)	(0.34)	(0.39)	(0.27)	(0.28)	(0.30)	(0.28)
Average age of funds (years)	3.42	3.72	3.63	4.00	4.58	5.37	6.10
	(2.07)	(2.30)	(2.58)	(2.82)	(2.94)	(3.05)	(3.30)
Average number of funds per adviser	7.89	8.82	9.16	10.58	11.99	13.81	16.36
	(5.24)	(6.58)	(8.44)	(8.68)	(11.16)	(14.03)	(17.61)
Percentage of broker-dealer funds	35.8	35.3	28.9	28.9	28.4	20.3	20.5

Note: Numbers in parentheses are standard deviations.
Source: Donoghue's Mutual Fund Almanac, 1980-1987 editions.

Table 6.2

Market Share Regression Estimates[a]

Independent variables[b]	(1)	(2)	(3)	(4)	(5)	(6)
Constant	0.24 (0.34)	0.24 (0.37)	-0.13 (-0.16)	-4.65 (-26.25)	-4.63 (-25.76)	-4.95 (-22.31)
Relative yield	23.86 (17.79)	20.38 (17.21)	22.21 (15.54)	23.52 (17.28)	20.52 (16.98)	22.43 (15.23)
Cross-product of yield and age	7.96 (5.21)	—	—	7.38 (4.76)	—	—
Number of funds in complex	0.40 (9.52)	0.43 (10.04)	0.66 (13.37)	0.03 (9.04)	0.04 (9.78)	0.05 (11.53)
Total number of retail, taxable funds	-1.54 (-11.23)	-1.54 (-11.07)	-1.61 (-9.53)	-0.02 (-11.31)	-0.02 (-11.29)	-0.02 (-9.48)
Broker affiliate	1.30 (14.43)	1.31 (14.19)	1.25 (11.23)	1.28 (14.04)	1.28 (13.86)	1.21 (10.51)

continued on next page

Table 6.2 continued

Independent variables[b]	(1)	(2)	(3)	(4)	(5)	(6)
R-squared	0.67	0.66	0.50	0.66	0.65	0.47
Adjusted R-squared	0.67	0.65	0.49	0.66	0.65	0.46
F-statistic	238.60	270.90	174.00	232.00	265.70	153.90

Notes: [a] t-statistics are given in parentheses.
[b] All variables are specified in their logarithmic form except for FUNDS and ALLDOM, which are given in their linear form in specifications 4, 5, and 6. BROKER is in linear form throughout.

For each set of estimates, as reported in Table 6.2, the coefficient of each of the independent variables has the expected sign, and are all highly statistically significant. In particular, we see that the market share of an MMF is higher (1) the more funds that are part of the complex, (2) the older the fund, and (3) if a fund has a broker/dealer affiliate.

For our purposes, by far the most striking feature of the results is the magnitude and statistical significance of the yield index variable. Since both the market share and yield index variables are expressed in logarithmic form, the coefficient of the yield index variable can be interpreted directly as the elasticity of market share with respect to net yield. Holding total market size constant, this same coefficient also represents the elasticity of fund demand with respect to net yield, since the percentage change in market share and percentage change in a fund's assets are identical. This interpretation holds for all the functional forms that are dealt with in Table 6.2, with the exception of the forms that include the cross-product of the age and yield index variables. This group of specifications aside, the elasticity estimates obtained range from 20.25 to 22.43. These results indicate that, other things being equal, a one percent decrease in the net yield of a fund relative to the average net yield of all funds in the sample will result in a reduction of over 20 percent in that fund's market share.

In the case of the regressions that include the cross-product of the yield and age variables, regressions (1) and (4), the computation of the elasticity is slightly more complicated, since it is a function of the relative age of a fund, which of course differs from one fund to another. Using the result of regression (1) in Table 6.2 as an illustration, the elasticity must satisfy the equation

$$\text{elasticity} = 23.86 + 7.96 \ln(\text{AGEIN}) \qquad (6.3)$$

so that for a fund of "average" age, i.e., AGEIN = 1, the elasticity is 23.9, while for a fund that is 25 percent older than average the elasticity rises to 25.6. Table 6.3 and Figure 6.2 describe the behavior over time of estimates of fund net yield

Table 6.3

Estimate of Fund Net Yield Elasticity

	1980	1981	1982	1983	1984	1985	1986
Elasticity First Quartile Age	19.6 0.59	18.92 0.54	13.6 0.28	18.42 0.5	17.29 0.44	19.23 0.56	20.51 0.66
Elasticity Median Age	22.83 0.88	22.14 0.81	22.34 0.83	21.64 0.76	22.81 0.88	21.52 0.74	22.29 0.82
Elasticity Third Quartile Age	25.12 1.17	27.66 1.61	27.86 1.65	27.16 1.51	26.04 1.31	25.97 1.3	26.02 1.31

Note: Net yield elasticity = 23.86 + [7.96 * ln(Age index)].
Source: Equation (1) in Table 6.2.

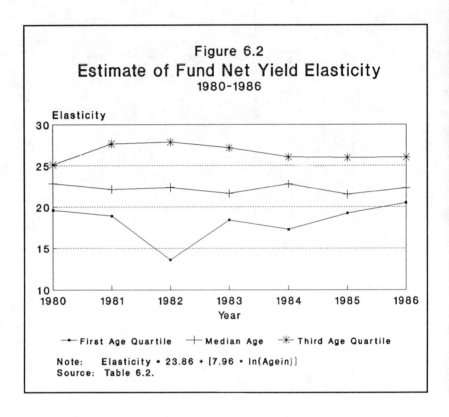

Figure 6.2
Estimate of Fund Net Yield Elasticity
1980-1986

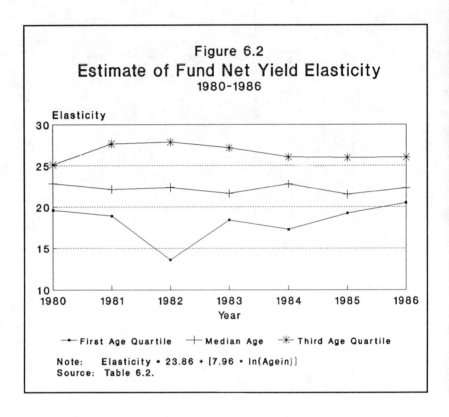

elasticity evaluated for several different fund age groups. The relative position of the three lines in the figure is influenced by the pattern of new fund entry in the 1980s. In years when new entry was significant, the three lines diverged because the average age in the lowest age quartile fell. For the same reason, for periods when the amount of new entry diminished, the lines tend to converge.

The dramatic implications of the estimated elasticities are shown in Figure 6.3, which is drawn on the assumption that the pertinent elasticity is 22.5. The figure shows the evolution of three hypothetical funds that start out in the base year with identical market shares of five percent. One fund is assumed to provide a net yield equal to the average net yield, while the other two funds deviate from the average by one percent, one

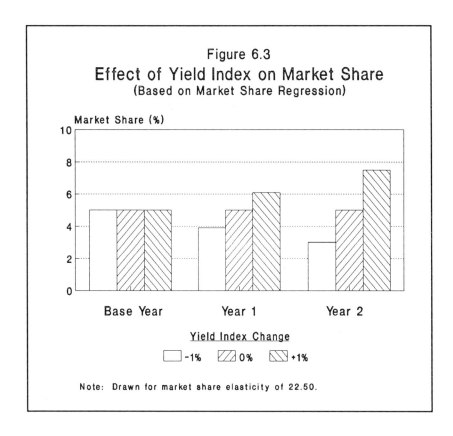

Figure 6.3
Effect of Yield Index on Market Share
(Based on Market Share Regression)

Note: Drawn for market share elasticity of 22.50.

in an upward direction and the other on the downside. That is, if the average net yield is eight percent, the low-yield fund is assumed to offer a return of seven percent and the high-yield fund a return of nine percent. After two years, the market share of the fund that offers a net yield below the average falls to 3.0 percent, while the share of the fund with a yield above the average rises to 7.5 percent. The results for a range of elasticities are reported in Table 6.4. In all cases, the substantial differences in market shares after two years attest to the considerable power of MMF shareholders to discipline those funds that offer relatively low net yields. Armed with this evidence, we can now turn to a discussion of fees.

Table 6.4

Effects of Yield on Market Share

	Deviation of Fund Yield from Base Yield		
	-1%	0%	1%
Elasticity = 20.00			
Market share (%)			
Base year	5.0	5.0	5.0
Year 1	4.0	5.0	6.0
Year 2	3.2	5.0	7.2
Elasticity = 22.50			
Market share (%)			
Base year	5.0	5.0	5.0
Year 1	3.9	5.0	6.1
Year 2	3.0	5.0	7.5
Elasticity = 25.00			
Market share (%)			
Base year	5.0	5.0	5.0
Year 1	3.8	5.0	6.3
Year 2	2.8	5.0	7.8

Fund Elasticity With Respect to Total Fees

Recall that the Appellate Court in *Gartenberg v. Merrill Lynch* argued that there could be vigorous competition among MMFs for shareholders and yet no competition for fund business among advisers. Earlier, we suggested that because of the direct effect of fees on net yields, a high degree of consumer sensitivity to net yield inevitably must impose some market discipline upon fee-setting behavior. Moreover, this must be true even if fees are relatively insignificant to many of the shareholders as long as they are sufficient to elicit a substantial response from the group as a whole. The elasticity estimates we obtained confirm that consumer sensitivity to net yields is substantial and, therefore, that implicit investor sensitivity to the level of fees is considerable. In fact, using our elasticity estimates, we can quantify the sensitivity of consumers to the level of fees by calculating the elasticity of the demand facing a money market fund with respect to fees charged by the fund.

Intuitively, it is clear that the greater the magnitude of the total fees in relation to the net income earned by the fund, the higher the elasticity with respect to fees. Of course, this elasticity is also higher the greater the underlying elasticity of demand with respect to net yield. These two relations can be combined in a single formula:

fee elasticity = (yield elasticity) x (fee ratio/net yield) (6.4)

where the fee ratio (or expense ratio) is the ratio of total fees to assets of the fund.[116] This formula can be used to calculate the elasticity with respect to the expense or fee ratio for each of the years in our sample, 1980-1986. The results of this exercise are shown in the third column of Table 6.5. For each year, the table also reports the average fee ratio and the average net yield. Estimates of demand elasticity with respect to the fee ratio range from 1.0 to 3.9.

As should be clear from the results, with the possible exception of 1981, the demand for MMFs is elastic with respect to the fee ratio (unity being the borderline between elasticity and inelasticity.) That is to say, a one percent rise in the relative fee charged by a fund adviser will lead to a more than proportionate loss in that fund's market share.

---

[116]This formula can be derived as follows. We rewrite equation (6.2) as $\ln(m) = a + b \ln(rg\text{-}f)$, where the net yield variable is expressed as the difference between the gross yield, rg, and the fee ratio, f, and where a combines all the other terms in (6.2). Equation (6.4) follows by differentiating with respect to f and rearranging the terms.

Table 6.5

Derived Demand Elasticity With Respect to Total Fees[a]

Year	Weighted average expense ratio	Average net yield	Derived demand elasticity[b]
1980	0.76	12.13	1.48
1981	0.72	17.09	1.00
1982	0.76	12.49	1.44
1983	0.81	8.66	2.21
1984	0.83	10.14	1.94
1985	0.87	7.71	2.67
1986	1.03	6.26	3.89

Notes: [a] Based on all retail, taxable, nongovernment money market funds.
[b] Derived demand elasticity is equal to 23.86 (Eq. (1) in Table 6.2) times the weighted average expense ratio over the average net yield.

Sources: Lipper — Directors' Analytical Data, February, 1980-1986 editions; Donoghue's Money Fund Report, December, 1980-1986 editions.

The reason demand with respect to fees was less elastic in 1981 can be seen by examining equation (6.4). Unusual market conditions resulted in an atypically high level of interest rates, including net yields on MMFs. Consequently, the fee ratio was unusually small in comparison with the net yield for 1981. This resulted in a lower fee elasticity for that year. Indeed, we can use equation (6.4) to solve for the minimum ratio of total fees to net income (which is identical to solving for the fee ratio divided by the net yield) above which fund demand with respect to the fee ratio is elastic. Minimum fee-net income figures that emerge can, perhaps, be interpreted as the borderline between the case where advisory fees are a "significant" component of the yield of a fund, and the case where they are "insignificant." The result depends, of course, on the underlying elasticity of fund demand with respect to net yield. If, for illustrative purposes, we take this elasticity to be

25 (which is well within the range of estimates yielded by our statistical calculations), then the critical ratio of fees to net income is .04. This means that if the fee ratio is 0.8, for example, the fund's net yield would have to exceed 20 percent to produce the inelastic case in which the fees can be deemed to be an insignificant share of the yield. Or, looked at the other way, if the net yield were as low as six percent (lower than the average figure for any of the years in the table), the fee ratio column(s) of the table would have to be less than .24 (a figure below any actually experienced) for inelasticity to arise.

Our methods probably underestimate investor sensitivity to fees for at least two important reasons. The first is due to the fact that we have restricted our sample to retail funds. Institutional investors, who are not included in our sample, are likely to be even more sensitive to net yield, and hence to fees, than the typical retail investor. Because their holdings are large, it pays them to monitor yield differences even more closely, and thus institutional investors will likely react to smaller yield differences more quickly than small retail investors.

The second reason stems from the fact that we have not captured variations in the services offered by different funds. The funds in our sample charge different fees. A plausible explanation for these differences is that funds that charge higher fees offer their customers more services, such as convenient telephone access to information and transactions, financial publications, and more complete documentation. Unfortunately, in our empirical analysis we were unable to include direct information on variations in the services offered by different funds. The consequence of this omission is likely to be an undervaluation of the elasticity of demand with respect to the net yield as well as to the fee ratio. Therefore, though our estimates of elasticity are high, they are probably conservative approximations of the true value.

Our analysis thus suggests that an advisory firm that sets its fees above competitive levels will almost always find itself losing substantially in terms of market share as investors shift their assets into other funds. Clearly, these findings establish that it is a mistake to base regulatory and judicial decisions on the premise that MMFs are not effectively constrained by market forces in their selection of fees.

SEVEN

A COST STUDY OF MUTUAL FUND COMPLEXES

INTRODUCTION

This chapter investigates the cost structure of mutual fund complexes. Views about the underlying cost structure, whether implicit or explicit, have shaped regulatory policies in a broad range of industries. A striking example of this influence is the regulation and subsequent deregulation in the telecommunications industry, where cost considerations played a major role.[117] Such considerations are also evident in policies toward mergers and in questions about appropriate lines of business for regulated firms.

Cost considerations have had a direct influence on the structure of the Investment Company Act and have been at the heart of various legal disputes involving fees charged by mutual fund advisers. As discussed in Chapter Two, the assumption that economies of scale are realized as the assets in a mutual fund grow had an important effect on the regulatory changes reflected in the 1970 Amendments to the Investment Company Act. Judicial opinions in litigation involving mutual funds consistently accepted the hypothesis that economies of scale are

---

[117] For a discussion of the role of cost considerations in the deregulation of the telecommunications industry, see Paul W. MacAvoy and Kenneth Robinson, "Winning by Losing: The AT&T Settlement and Its Impact on Telecommunications," *Yale Journal on Regulation*, vol. 1, no. 1 (1983), 1-42.

present. However, neither the litigants involved in excess fee cases nor the 1960s' studies of the mutual fund industry have presented a systematic treatment of this issue.

Since the cost structure of a fund cannot be analyzed by considering the fund in isolation, the absence of a rigorous treatment is not surprising. Rather, one must directly address the measurement and interpretation problems posed by the multiproduct nature of the mutual fund complex. Put another way, analysis of scale economies requires consideration of the production technology and the costs faced by the mutual fund complex as a whole and not just the costs attributed to a single fund. The purpose of this chapter is to estimate the cost function of mutual fund complexes. By explicitly taking into account the multiproduct nature of the mutual fund complex, we are able to address questions of economies of scale in a defensible manner. Also, estimation of the cost function will allow us to determine whether groups of products exhibit economies of scope. This will help us to determine whether the horizontal structures of firms in the mutual fund industry are motivated by efficiency considerations or by other goals that are less consistent with social interests.

Cost functions can play other useful roles in addition to permitting the examination of scale and scope economies. In particular, we saw earlier that the incremental cost test is an important component of any proper evaluation of a claim that excessive fees have been charged or excessive profits earned by an adviser of a mutual fund. Explicit analysis of the cost function of the mutual fund complex is one way in which such an incremental cost test can be carried out for a particular fund whose fees have been challenged.

Finally, knowledge of cost functions is useful for public policy discussions of the mutual fund industry. For example, it was recently reported that the SEC was undertaking a review of the costs of mutual funds, but was doing so by examining the ratio of expenses to assets for various categories of mutual funds.[118] While this is certainly a reasonable first step, the SEC's objective can be pursued more effectively by estimation of a cost function. This would allow one to build explicitly into the model the dependence of a fund's expense ratio on the quantity of the assets managed by the firm, and also on variables such as measures of fund activity and fund attributes.

The remainder of this chapter is divided into four sections. The first section discusses cost functions for a multiproduct firm. The second section provides a detailed description of the empirical analysis and includes a description of the data and functional form we have used to estimate the cost function of mutual fund complexes. The third section presents the econometric results, including estimates of overall economies of scale and scope. The final section presents the conclusions derived from the analysis.

COST FUNCTIONS

The cost function, together with the closely related concept of the production function, are two ways of describing the production technology of a firm. These concepts apply to both single product and multiproduct firms, and to illustrate the basic ideas we begin with the former case.

While the production function relates the quantities of the inputs used in the production process to the resultant level of output, the cost function expresses the relationship between a firm's total costs and the quantities of the outputs that are produced. Since it is possible to produce a given set of outputs at different total costs, it is important to emphasize that a basic assumption underlying a firm's cost function is that production is carried out in the most efficient, i.e., the cost-minimizing, manner. For example, a cost function for McDonald's assumes that the firm hires and allocates its labor in a cost-minimizing, or efficient, manner. Naturally, the costs of producing a given

---

[118] Michael Siconolfi, "SEC is Studying Cost Differences of Mutual Funds," *The Wall Street Journal* (June 22, 1988), 37.

level of output depend on the firm's production technology as well as on the price of inputs. Hence, input prices are regarded as variables of the cost function.

Provided that certain conditions are met, the firm's production function can be derived from its cost function.[119] In other words, the cost function is simply another means of characterizing the production technology of the firm. The relationship between the production function and cost function is perhaps best illustrated with reference to the concept of returns to scale, which describes the response of output to a proportionate increase in all inputs. A firm is said to exhibit economies of scale or increasing returns to scale when increasing each input by some proportionate amount leads to a greater than proportionate increase in output. For example, if a firm were to increase its employment of each input by 10 percent and as a result output were able to increase by 12 percent, then the firm's production would be said to exhibit economies of scale with scale elasticity of 1.2 (12/10). If output increases in exact proportion to the increase in inputs, the firm's production is said to display constant returns to scale. Finally, if the percentage increase in output is less than the increase in input quantities that brings it about, the firm is said to exhibit decreasing returns to scale or diseconomies of scale.[120]

Although economies of scale clearly are a property of the production function, they also are reflected in the firm's cost function. To understand this relationship, it is helpful to consider the concept of output cost elasticity, which is defined

---

[119] The link between production technology and the cost function is termed *duality*. The production function indicates the maximum outputs attainable with given input quantities. The cost function yields the minimum cost of producing a specified output level. The two approaches are equivalent. For a thorough treatment of duality, see H.R. Varian, *Microeconomic Analysis* (New York: W.W. Norton and Co., 1978).

[120] The degree of economies of scale depends on the firm's production level. Typically, a firm enjoys relatively greater economies of scale at low output levels, and as output increases, economies of scale diminish so that eventually the firm experiences diseconomies of scale.

as the percentage change in the total costs of a firm divided by the associated percentage change in output that gave rise to the change in costs. If the output cost elasticity is less than unity, the firm exhibits economies of scale, or increasing returns to scale. Put another way, if technology is such that costs of production increase proportionately less than output as output increases, the firm exhibits economies of scale. Indeed, the scale elasticity, which is the measure of economies of scale, is simply the inverse of the output cost elasticity. An output cost elasticity exceeding unity implies diseconomies of scale, or decreasing returns to scale. That is, average costs rise with output expansion. We now need to see how this notion generalizes to the multiproduct firm.

As suggested earlier, almost all firms produce a variety of outputs, which have different qualities or attributes. This is certainly true of mutual fund complexes, which not only operate a number of different funds but are often part of a larger financial institution that offers a variety of financial intermediary services. These services can include, for example, brokerage services, private money management, or insurance products. Estimation of a cost function for such complexes requires explicit recognition of the multiproduct character of the production process.[121] Fortunately, there is a substantial literature extending the notion of the cost function to the multiproduct firm.[122] The cost function of a multiproduct firm

---

[121] Note that early studies in the banking industry aggregated banks' outputs into a single index. See, for example, M. Flannery, "Correspondent Services and Cost Economies in Commercial Banking," unpublished manuscript, University of Pennsylvania (1981); and G.J. Benston, G. Hanweck, and D. Humphrey, "Scale Economies in Banking: A Restructuring and Reassessment," *Journal of Money, Credit and Banking*, vol. 14 (November, 1982), 435-456.

[122] Studies that deal explicitly with the multiproduct nature of a firm's output include W.J. Baumol, "On the Proper Tests for Natural Monopoly in a Multiproduct Industry," *American Economic Review*, vol. 67 (December, 1977), 809-822; John C. Panzar and Robert D. Willig, "Economies of Scope," *AEA Papers and Proceedings* (May, 1981), 268-272; R.H. Spady and A.F. Friedlaender, "Hedonic Cost Functions for the Regulated Trucking Industry,"

expresses total costs as a function of each of the outputs produced by the firm and their unique attributes.

In the multiproduct firm, some care must be exercised in testing for the presence of scale economies. In particular, measures of product-specific economies of scale are difficult to define clearly when a firm produces more than one output.[123] However, it is possible to measure the magnitude of overall economies of scale by means of an analysis of the behavior of total costs as all outputs are increased in proportion. Suppose, for example, that all outputs of a firm were to increase by a given percentage. If the resultant percentage increase in total costs is less than the corresponding percentage increase in outputs, then the firm is said to exhibit overall economies of scale. While this definition is the natural generalization of the output cost elasticity of the single product firm, its interpretation requires care since its formulation is based on a hypothetical increase in all outputs of the firm by exactly the same percentage and fixed input prices. Nevertheless, measures of overall returns to scale provide a useful summary statistic, especially in comparison with returns to scale obtained from an aggregate production or cost function derived by combining all outputs into a single variable. We report on various measures of overall returns to scale below.

While the notion of economies of scale applies to both single product and multiproduct firms, the concept of economies of scope, alluded to earlier, is one that only takes on meaning in a multiproduct setting. More particularly, if the technology is truly a multiproduct one, then it is apt to be more efficient to produce several outputs together than to employ

---

Bell Journal of Economics, vol. 9 (Spring, 1978), 159-179; and M. Fuss and L. Waverman, "Regulation and the Multiproduct Firm: The Case of Telecommunications in Canada," G. Fromm, ed., *Studies in Public Regulation* (Cambridge: MIT Press, 1981).

[123] See the discussion in W.J. Baumol, J. Panzar, and R. Willig, *Contestable Markets and the Theory of Market Structure* (New York: Harcourt, Brace & Jovanovich, 1982). For a more pessimistic view, see M. Fuss and L. Waverman, op. cit.

separate production processes. That is, in a true multiproduct
environment, firms can realize cost savings by producing several
outputs jointly rather than specializing in the production of any
single output. It is these efficiency gains or cost savings that
are known as economies of scope. Economies of scope
typically arise from the joint usage of a fixed resource. For
example, in a mutual fund complex, if several funds are able to
use a common computer network and telecommunications
systems, then economies of scope are likely to result. In
practical applications, one does not simply assume that
economies of scope are present. Rather, one can explicitly test
for the existence of such savings by performing statistical tests
on the extent of *jointness* exhibited by the production
technology. The results of these tests are reported later in this
chapter, while the technical details are reported in Appendix C.

Explicit estimation of a cost function that takes into
account the multiproduct nature of the firm's production avoids
the arbitrariness that often besets a cost-disaggregation process
when a firm produces two or more outputs. Such situations
frequently give rise to joint or common costs, no proportion of
which can, even in principle, be attributed uniquely to any
individual output of the firm. Despite the resulting and
inherent impossibility of estimating the share of the firm's total
cost attributable to one of a firm's several products, attempts
are frequently made to do so. The most common type of
calculation relies on arbitrary allocations, and is referred to as
fully distributed cost. The estimation of a multiproduct cost
function permits direct analysis of the characteristics of a firm's
technology and avoids the need for arbitrary allocations.

EMPIRICAL ANALYSIS

This section describes the empirical analysis used to estimate a hedonic cost function for mutual fund complexes.[124] The hedonic cost function takes into account not only the levels of outputs, but also the characteristics of those outputs. Estimation of the cost function for mutual fund complexes requires a number of simplifying assumptions. Among the most critical is the assumption pertaining to non-mutual fund activities within the complex. Recall that it is very common for a mutual fund complex to be part of a larger organization that provides a range of financial services. However, because systematic data on the non-mutual fund activities were not available, we had no choice but to disregard non-mutual fund activity within a complex. This omission is an issue to the extent that cost complementarities exist between the mutual fund activities of a complex and its other operations, but there is no reason to believe that this omission introduces any obvious bias into the study. Clearly, future research may center on examining this issue.

Three other sets of assumptions critical to the analysis are made. The first deals with output definition in the mutual fund complex. The second deals with the set of hedonics used to capture the characteristics of output. The third relates to the measurement of the total costs of the complex. The treatment of these issues is described below.

---

[124] A hedonic cost function is one that contains variables that describe or otherwise characterize the firm's outputs. For example, Friedlaender, Winston, and Wang use cylinder capacity as a hedonic variable to describe the output of auto manufacturers. See A.F. Friedlaender, C. Winston, and K. Wang, "Costs, Technology, and Productivity in the U.S. Automobile Industry," *Bell Journal of Economics*, vol. 14 (Spring, 1983), 1-20. Presumably, more inputs are consumed in producing cars with larger cylinder capacity than in smaller-cylinder-capacity cars. The use of the term *hedonic* for this purpose seems to have been introduced by Court (1939). See A.T. Court, *The Dynamics of Automobile Demand* (New York: General Motors Corporation, 1939).

Output Measures and Choice of Hedonic Variables

The appropriate definition of output is critical for estimation of the cost function of a mutual fund complex. Numerous studies have reported cost functions for nonfinancial firms that generally produce fairly well-defined outputs, such as automobiles (Friedlaender, Winston, and Wang, 1983), journals (Baumol and Braunstein, 1977), and trucking (Spady and Friedlaender, 1978). In contrast, in the relatively few studies of financial service institutions, output definition is typically much less straightforward.[125]

Two studies that do provide some guidance have been reported by Murray and White (1983) and Gilligan, Smirlock, and Marshall (1984), who estimate cost functions for the banking industry. In their study of credit unions in British Columbia, Murray and White take the dollar value of earning assets as the output measure. They also try an alternative specification, taking the number of accounts as the output, and find that the results are not sensitive to the choice of output measure. Murray and White include a number of hedonic variables in the cost function. The variables measure growth, risk, the number of branch offices, and average account size. Gilligan et al., in their study of commercial banking, measure outputs by the volume of deposits and loans, but also include average deposit size and average loan size as hedonic variables.

What constitutes output in the context of a mutual fund complex is ambiguous. Following the previously cited research, we alternatively consider assets and number of accounts as the output measures.[126] Output definition is further complicated by

---

[125] For a recent review of cost studies of depository financial institutions, see J.A. Clark, "Economies of Scale and Scope at Depository Financial Institutions," *Economic Review*, Federal Reserve Bank of Kansas City, vol. 73, no. 8 (September/October, 1988), 16-33.

[126] There is something curious about this choice of output measures, since one may view these as inputs in the production of returns. Nevertheless, the traditional approach is to regard these as outputs and to regard as inputs labor, capital, and similar factors of production.

aggregation issues. Specifically, while assets and number of accounts may seem reasonable units in which to measure output, they do not provide the basis for aggregation of funds within a complex into discrete products. We have chosen to compute output for two product types, money market funds and non-money market funds. For example, when assets are selected as the output measure, we define assets in money market funds and assets in other funds as the pertinent outputs. We also experimented with aggregation of outputs into three groups: money market funds, fixed income funds, and other funds. The results obtained from this finer division were not very different from those obtained from the money market/ non-money market division that are reported here; thus, we opted for the more parsimonious specification.

Table 7.1 summarizes the output measures and hedonic variables used in the cost estimation models. As the table shows, there are four basic specifications, two of which measure output by assets while the other two measure outputs by the number of accounts. The hedonic variables always include the number of money market funds and non-money market funds in the complex and the portfolio turnover rate for other funds.[127] In the models where the number of accounts is taken as the output, assets or assets per account are also included as hedonic variables. When assets are considered the outputs, either the number of accounts or the assets per account are included as hedonic variables. The distinction between the inclusion of the number of accounts as against the assets per account as hedonic variables centers on the effect on measurement of economies of scale. When measuring economies of scale in models that use assets per account as the hedonic variable, the implicit assumption is that assets and accounts change in fixed proportions. On the other hand, when assets or number of accounts is the hedonic variable, the

---

[127] Portfolio turnover rate is defined as the minimum of purchases and sales divided by net average assets. Since money market funds typically hold short-term assets until maturity, sales are zero. As a result, the turnover rate is almost always zero, and is not included in our model specifications.

Table 7.1

Output and Hedonic Variables in Regression Models

	Output	
	Assets	Number of accounts
Hedonic variables	Number of accounts Number of funds Portfolio turnover rate	Assets Number of funds Portfolio turnover rate
	Assets per account Number of funds Portfolio turnover rate	Assets per account Number of funds Portfolio turnover rate

Model Specifications

In our analysis we have used a translog cost function to represent costs in a mutual fund complex. The translog cost function is quadratic in logarithms. Because of its unrestrictive nature and flexibility, the translog cost function has often been used in econometric applications since its introduction in the early 1970s.[129]

The chief advantage of the translog cost specification is that it can approximate any arbitrarily selected cost function. Previously, researchers generally based their analyses on restrictive functional forms, such as the Cobb-Douglas function, which may be inappropriate. Further, the properties of translog cost functions are such that restrictions implicitly imposed on the production technology are consistent with profit-maximizing behavior. Additional advantages relate to the computational ease of obtaining measures of overall economies of scale and economies of scope, and the relatively small number of parameters to be estimated in contrast with other approaches.[130] The translog relationship used to estimate the cost function of mutual fund complexes is of the following general form:

$$\ln(C) = a_0 + \sum_i a_i \ln(y_i) + \sum_i \sum_j d_{ij} \ln(y_i)\ln(y_j)$$

$$+ \sum_i \sum_j b_{ij} \ln(h_{ij}), \tag{7.1}$$

---

[129] For an early treatment of translog cost functions in econometric applications, see L.R. Christensen, D.W. Jorgenson, and L.J. Lau, "Transcendental Logarithmic Production Functions," *Review of Economics and Statistics*, vol. 55 (January, 1973), 28-45. For a more recent discussion, see D.W. Jorgenson, "Econometric Methods for Modeling Producer Behavior," *Handbook of Econometrics*, vol. 3, Z. Griliches and M. Intriligator, eds. (Amsterdam: North Holland, 1986).

[130] For further discussion and clarification of these points, see D.W. Caves, L.R. Christensen, and M.W. Tretheway, "Flexible Cost Functions for Multiproduct Firms," *Review of Economics and Statistics*, vol. 62 (August, 1980), 477-481.

where

$$C = \text{complex costs,}$$
$$y_i = \text{output } i,$$
$$h_{ij} = \text{hedonic variable } j \text{ describing output } i,$$
$$a_0, a_i, d_{ij}, b_{ij} = \text{parameters to be estimated.}$$

The inclusion of hedonic variables is a variation on traditional translog cost models. The original studies that estimated translog cost models did not include hedonic terms (e.g., Christensen, Jorgenson, and Lau, 1973, and Fuss and Waverman, 1981); however, over time hedonics have been introduced into the functional form (e.g., Spady and Friedlaender, 1978, and Murray and White, 1983) as it was recognized that particular characteristics of output are systematically related to costs. In the context of mutual fund complexes, the inclusion of the number of accounts as a hedonic variable in several of the specifications that we estimated is explained by the conjecture that this is an important measure of the underlying transaction activity within a fund. This activity, in turn, can be expected to have a direct effect on total complex costs. For example, consider two money market funds with similar amounts of assets under management. All else being equal, one would expect the fund with more accounts to have more transactions activity and, therefore, to incur greater costs.

A key difference between the general formulation of the cost function we have used and that employed in most previous studies is the absence of input shares and input prices. Because of the lack of publicly available data on factor inputs and factor prices for each complex, we are unable to estimate the cost function using the more general approach.[131] As a result of this limitation, we cannot to investigate certain

---

[131] The more general approach would estimate the cost function simultaneously with factor share equations, and the factor prices would appear directly in the cost function.

properties of the production technology, such as elasticities of substitution between inputs. In addition, our estimation techniques necessarily are less efficient than those that take advantage of information on input prices and shares.

Description of Data and Complex Selection Criteria

The primary data sources for the cost analysis are the annual *Directors' Reports*, published by Lipper Analytical Services, Inc., for the years 1982 through 1987. For each fund within a complex, these reports contain data on the fund's advisory and nonadvisory expenses as well as on additional items, such as net sales, average net assets, fund objective, and portfolio turnover rate over the period corresponding to the fund's most recently completed fiscal year.

For the years 1982 to 1987, the complete universe of funds reported in *Lipper's Directors' Reports* contains an average of 1,186 funds and 257 complexes per year. If all the data were usable, we would have 1,542 complex-year observations (6 x 257). The actual sample used to estimate the cost function of mutual fund complexes is substantially smaller for a variety of reasons, the single most important being incomplete data. A large number of funds did not report information for all of the variables of interest in our analysis. Rather than remove all complexes having funds with any missing data, we removed a complex from the sample only if the funds with missing data compose more than a certain percentage of the complex's total assets. We used two filter levels: a five percent and 40 percent cutoff. Under a five percent cutoff, for example, if more than five percent of the complex's assets were in funds with missing data, the complex was removed for that year.[132]

We used another filter that is related to the treatment of complexes that perform only administrative or only advisory roles for a given fund. Because it is not clear how the costs associated with such funds should be divided between the

---

[132] Regression results from the 40 percent filter are found in Appendix B.

administering and advising complexes, we excluded funds having a separate administrator and adviser and retained in the sample only complexes where the assets of the administer-only and advise-only funds account for less than a preselected percentage of the complex's total assets. As before, we use filter levels of five percent and 40 percent.[133] Overall, with the five percent filters, incomplete data accounted for the loss of two thirds of our potential observations.[134]

Table 7.2 presents summary statistics describing the 179 observations selected via the five percent filter. Over the entire sample period, average complex expenses were $9,503,000, and mean net average assets were $1,295 million, which translates to an average expense-asset ratio of 0.73 percent. Average assets invested in non-money market funds over the sample period were nearly twice the assets under management in money market funds. As the data in Appendix A show, the relative share of assets invested in non-MMFs increased in later years because of the considerable growth in equity and growth funds. On the other hand, the average account size was greater in money market funds ($13,461) than for non-money market funds ($9,220). This relationship persisted in most of the sample years.

Finally, it should be noted that total costs, which constitute the dependent variable of the regression equations, include all profits as well as labor and real capital expenses. This approach was used largely because of data limitations but is similar to that adopted by Murray and White (1983), who treat all distributed profits as costs. Also note that in the regression analysis, assets, number of accounts, and assets per

---

[133] Note that we only use the five percent missing data filter with the five percent administer-only/advise-only filter. That is, we do not use a five percent filter in conjunction with a 40 percent filter.

[134] The specific effects in terms of the selection criteria are presented more fully in Appendix A. As noted there, the inability of the translog specification to accommodate zero output levels also reduced the number of usable observations as complexes offering only one output type were removed from the sample.

Table 7.2

Complexes Offering Both Outputs, 179 Observations, Five Percent Filter

Variable	Minimum	Maximum	Mean
Total expenses ($ thousands)	450	67,245	9,503
Money market assets ($ thousands)	1,390	6,220,750	468,250
Other fund assets ($ thousands)	6,290	9,522,900	826,620
Money market assets per account ($)	2,078	48,223	13,461
Other fund assets per account ($)	1,528	43,403	9,220
Number of money market accounts	117	448,479	36,843
Number of other fund accounts	578	943,365	90,699
Number of money market funds	1.00	4.00	1.32
Number of other funds	1.00	18.00	4.76
Other fund turnover (%)	3.00	264.04	75.32

Note: All dollar amounts are expressed in 1986 constant dollars using
        the GNP deflator.

account are always normalized to have a mean of one. This is a standard approach designed to facilitate the computation of overall economies of scale and economies of scope.[135]

ECONOMETRIC RESULTS

Tables 7.3 through 7.6 present the parameter estimates and other statistics for the four specifications of the cost function. All specifications fit the data extremely well, as is indicated by adjusted R^2s that all exceed 0.97. However, high R^2s provide no guarantee that the estimated models make economic sense. Rather, one needs to examine the signs and statistical significance of the key coefficients.

---

[135] We should also note that in estimation we have imposed the restriction that $d_{12} = d_{21}$, a symmetry condition necessary for the conventional interpretation of the translog cost function. On this and the issue of normalization, see Fuss and Waverman, op. cit.

Table 7.3

Estimation of Cost Function

Output   = Assets
Hedonics = Number of accounts, number of funds, portfolio turnover
Filter   = Five percent

Variable	Coefficient	t-value
Intercept	15.654	200.94
ln(MM assets)	0.268	8.16
ln(Other assets)	0.299	10.43
ln(Number of MM accounts)	0.140	4.47
ln(Number of other accounts)	0.149	5.50
ln(Number of MM funds)	0.011	0.27
ln(Number of other funds)	0.220	6.43
ln(Turnover)	0.017	1.09
$[\ln(\text{MM assets})]^2$	0.090	20.61
$[\ln(\text{Other assets})]^2$	0.070	14.22
ln(MM assets) x ln(Other assets)	-0.133	-21.66
Number of observations:	179	
Adjusted R-sq.:	0.979	

Table 7.4

Estimation of Cost Function

Output   = Assets
Hedonics = Assets per account, number of funds, portfolio turnover
Filter   = Five percent

Variable	Coefficient	t-value
Intercept	15.644	200.94
ln(MM assets)	0.407	24.53
ln(Other assets)	0.448	23.28
ln(MM assets per account)	-0.140	-4.47
ln(Other assets per account)	-0.149	-5.50
ln(Number of MM funds)	0.011	0.27
ln(Number of other funds)	0.220	6.43
ln(Turnover)	0.017	1.09
$[\ln(\text{MM assets})]^2$	0.090	20.61
$[\ln(\text{Other assets})]^2$	0.070	14.22
ln(MM assets) x ln(Other assets)	-0.133	-21.66
Number of observations:	179	
Adjusted R-sq.:	0.979	

Table 7.5

Estimation of Cost Function

Output   = Number of accounts
Hedonics = Assets, number of funds, portfolio turnover
Filter   = Five percent

Variable	Coefficient	t-value
Intercept	15.712	191.77
ln(MM assets)	0.205	6.36
ln(Other assets)	0.243	8.28
ln(Number of MM accounts)	0.153	4.22
ln(Number of other accounts)	0.270	7.63
ln(Number of MM funds)	0.072	1.75
ln(Number of other funds)	0.101	2.77
ln(Turnover)	0.055	3.39
$[\ln(\text{No. of MM accounts})]^2$	0.073	15.65
$[\ln(\text{No. of other accounts})]^2$	0.081	15.80
ln(No. MM accts) x ln(No. other accts)	-0.143	-21.13
Number of observations:	179	
Adjusted R-sq.:	0.977	

Table 7.6

Estimation of Cost Function

Output   = Number of accounts
Hedonics = Assets per account, number of funds, portfolio turnover
Filter   = Five percent

Variable	Coefficient	t-value
Intercept	15.726	191.69
ln(MM assets per account)	0.205	6.36
ln(Other assets per account)	0.243	8.28
ln(Number of MM accounts)	0.358	20.38
ln(Number of other accounts)	0.513	23.54
ln(Number of MM funds)	0.072	1.75
ln(Number of other funds)	0.101	2.77
ln(Turnover)	0.005	3.39
$[\ln(\text{No. of MM accounts})]^2$	0.073	15.65
$[\ln(\text{No. of other accounts})]^2$	0.081	15.80
ln(No. MM accts) x ln(No. other accts)	-0.143	-21.13
Number of observations:	179	
Adjusted R-sq.:	0.977	

The output variables, which are the primary variables of interest, enter the translog specification in three distinct ways: linearly, in quadratic form, and as cross-products of a money market output variable with a non-money market output variable. In all specifications, the linear and quadratic terms are positive, as is to be expected, and all are statistically significant. The coefficients of the cross-product of the output variables have the expected negative sign and are also strongly significant. This, of course, is a necessary condition for there to be economies of scope but, as we shall see, is not sufficient. When assets are taken as the output measure, the results indicate that as the number of accounts increases, costs also increase. The results also suggest that increases in the number of funds within a complex are associated with increased costs. However, in the case of money market funds, the estimated coefficient is not statistically significant.

When assets are taken to be the output variable and assets per account the hedonic, the estimates imply that an increase in assets per account leads to a decrease in costs. The reason for this is that an increase in assets per account with a fixed total quantity of assets must entail a decrease in the number of accounts, an occurrence that can be expected to reduce total costs.

Ambiguous results were obtained for the turnover variable. While the estimated coefficients for the turnover variable have their expected sign — i.e., they imply that a rise in turnover increases costs — the coefficients are statistically significant only when the number of accounts is taken as the output variable.

Economies of Scale and Scope

As discussed previously, a generalization of the single-output cost elasticity is used to evaluate whether or not overall

economies of scale are present.[136]   To examine overall economies of scale, we use the multiproduct output cost elasticity.[137]
This measure has the following properties: if it is less than
one, we say there are overall economies of scale; if it equals
one, we say there are constant (overall) returns to scale; and if
it is greater than one, we say there are overall diseconomies of
scale. We compute this measure at both the average sample
output levels, and the observed output level for each complex.

Table 7.7 presents estimates of the overall economies of
scale evaluated at the sample mean and at each complex's
actual output levels for the four model specifications. In all
cases, overall economies of scale are present and statistically
significant, but the magnitude of the output cost elasticity
depends on the individual model specification. In particular,
the estimates indicate that whenever assets per account are
considered a hedonic variable, regardless of how output is
measured, the output cost elasticity is much closer to unity.
For example, when output is measured by assets and the
hedonic given by assets per account, the output cost elasticity
is 0.855. On the other hand, if the hedonic is the number of
accounts, the output cost elasticity is a substantially smaller
0.566. The intuitive explanation of such a result depends on
the assumptions implicit in the use of assets per account as
opposed to the number of accounts as a hedonic variable. In
the former case, the implicit assumption is that as assets,
money market and other, increase by a proportion, the number
of accounts increases by the same proportion. On the other
hand, with the inclusion of number of accounts, the implicit
assumption is that as assets increase by a proportion, the
number of accounts remains constant. Since we saw that
increases in assets as well as in the number of accounts are

---

[136] See Appendix C for a formal derivation of the measures and statistical
tests discussed in this section.

[137] Some researchers, e.g., Fuss and Waverman, op. cit., use the reciprocal
of the multiproduct output cost elasticity. Regardless of which measure is
computed, the economic implications are unaltered.

Table 7.7

Overall Economies of Scale, Five Percent Filter

Model specification	Measure of overall economies of scale			
	At average output levels (t-statistic)[a]	Median value	Complexes with significant overall economies of scale[b]	Complexes with significant overall diseconomies of scale[b]
Output = Assets Hedonic = Number of accounts	0.566 (-10.828)	0.519	179	0
Output = Assets Hedonic = Assets per account	0.855 (-7.200)	0.807	174	0
Output = Number of accounts Hedonic = Assets	0.423 (-14.252)	0.400	179	0
Output = Number of accounts Hedonic = Assets per account	0.871 (-6.200)	0.847	178	0

Notes: All models include number of funds and turnover rate as additional hedonic variables.
[a] t-statistics, computed for the measure of overall economies of scale, test whether constant returns to scale are present.
[b] Significance is determined using a five percent level.

both associated with increased costs, the results obtained are not surprising.

Overall economies of scale were also evaluated at the output levels of individual observations in the sample. For essentially all observations in each of the four specifications, there were statistically significant overall scale economies. Since production techniques often exhibit diminishing returns to scale as output increases, it is of interest to analyze whether the degree to which economies of scale are present is related to the level of output. One means of detecting such a relationship is by computing the rank correlations between the measure of overall economies of scale with the output measure. The rank correlation between overall economies of scale and total net assets, for example, allows one to assess statistically whether complexes that exhibit relatively greater economies of scale tend to be complexes with relatively greater or smaller total net assets.[138]

Table 7.8 presents rank correlations of overall economies of scale with the two output measures, assets and accounts, where the output measures have been summed over fund types. For all model specifications, the greater the output, whether interpreted as number of accounts or net assets, the smaller the degree of overall scale economies. The positive rank correlation given in Table 7.8 stems from the use of the output cost elasticity as a measure of overall economies of scale. Moreover, the rank correlation between overall economies of scale and the output measure is always statistically significant. Intuitively, this makes sense and is consistent with generally observed characteristics of actual production processes.

---

[138] In computing a rank correlation, the values of the two variables to be correlated are replaced by their relative ranks (highest number, second-highest number, etc.). A rank correlation simply correlates the rank of one variable with that of another.

Table 7.8

Rank Correlation of Overall Economies of Scale and Scope with Output Measures, Five Percent Filter

Model specification	With:	Rank correlation of overall economies of scale		With:	Rank correlation of economies of scope	
		Total assets	Number of accounts		Total assets	Number of accounts
Output = Assets Hedonics = Number of accounts		0.831 (*)	0.732 (*)		0.333 (*)	0.362 (*)
Output = Assets Hedonics = Assets per account		0.831 (*)	0.732 (*)		0.414 (*)	0.434 (*)
Output = Number of accounts Hedonics = Assets		0.789 (*)	0.906 (*)		0.106	0.107
Output = Number of accounts Hedonics = Assets per account		0.789 (*)	0.906 (*)		0.237 (*)	0.240 (*)

Note: (*) denotes significant at five percent level.

Economies of scope were evaluated at sample average output levels as well as for each complex.[139] Measures of economies of scope are presented in Table 7.9. The estimated presence or absence of economies of scope between MMFs and other funds depends on both the model specification and the point selected for evaluation. Whenever assets per account were not included as hedonic variables (first and third models), economies of scope were unambiguously detected and were statistically significant, both at the means and for essentially all individual complex observations. In the two specifications that included assets per account as a hedonic variable, the results obtained are less clear. Although there are no economies of scope at the sample means — indeed, there appear to be diseconomies — 34 percent to 45 percent of the individual complexes in the sample display statistically significant economies of scope while 29 percent display significant diseconomies of scope. Of course, diseconomies of scope are inconsistent with a true underlying joint production process. As a consequence, the existence of apparent diseconomies of scope when assets per account serves as the hedonic variable suggests a misspecification of the cost function. More particularly, it suggests that the preferred specification is one which uses the number of accounts (or assets) as a hedonic.

Rank correlations between the output measures and economies of scope are also presented in Table 7.8. The correlations are positive and statistically significant except for the model specification with number of accounts as the output variable and assets as a hedonic variable. In the case of economies of scope, a positive rank correlation indicates that complexes with relatively low output tend to have relatively greater economies of scope, because economies of scope are

---

[139] As shown in Appendix C, when economies of scope are evaluated at the sample means and when the values of the output variables have been normalized, the expression for economies of scope is given by $a_1 a_2 + d_{12}$ (using the notation in equation (7.1)). Economies of scope are said to exist when the resultant measure is negative. Computing economies of scope for each complex requires the transformation of the estimated coefficients, which is also described in Appendix C.

Table 7.9

Economies of Scope, Five Percent Filter

Model specification scope[b]	At average output levels (t-statistic)[a]	Measure of economies of scope		
		Median value	Complexes with significant economies of scope[b]	Complexes with significant diseconomies of scope
Output = Assets Hedonic = Number of accounts	-0.053 (-3.753)	-0.104	177	0
Output = Assets Hedonic = Assets per account	0.049 (4.664)	-0.012	81	52
Output = Number of accounts Hedonic = Assets	-0.102 (-8.755)	-0.136	179	0
Output = Number of accounts Hedonic = Assets per account	0.040 (3.577)	0.006	61	52

Notes: All models include number of funds and turnover rate as additional hedonic variables.
[a] t-statistics, computed for the measure of overall economies of scale, test whether constant returns to scale are present.
[b] Significance is determined using a five percent level.

present when the statistic is negative. Thus, there appears to be an incentive for complexes to offer funds of both types even when the complexes are small.

CONCLUSIONS

The results of the econometric analysis of mutual fund complexes' costs have important policy implications for the treatment of fees that mutual fund managers charge. As we have seen, the presumption that mutual funds exhibit economies of scale as the assets under management grow has played a critical role in both the formulation of policy and the courts' evaluation of allegations that fees are excessive. However, while assumptions about the behavior of costs have had a direct influence on both policy decisions and judicial opinions, no direct empirical evidence has been offered on the nature of the costs incurred by a mutual fund complex.

Estimation of the cost function for a mutual fund complex poses several difficult problems that do not typically beset cost estimation for other types of products and services. This difficulty is particularly true of output definition. Previous treatments of mutual fund costs have assumed assets under management to be the unit of output.[140] Our analysis, on the other hand, suggests that measurement of output involves complicated issues and that the best procedure ultimately depends on the questions that are being addressed. For a mutual fund complex, it makes perfect sense to ask what would happen to costs if either accounts or assets in the complex were to increase. The empirical analysis we have conducted allows us to address both those inquiries.

Our results indicate the presence of overall economies of scale in mutual fund complexes. While this finding is independent of output measure and choice of hedonic variable, the degree that overall economies of scale are present depends

---

[140] For examples, see *Saxe v. Brady, Acampora v. Birkland*, and *SEC Policy Report*, op. cit.

on the cost function specified. There is a sensitivity to the choice of output, and more critically to the choice of hedonics. In particular, whenever assets per account are included as hedonic variables, overall economies of scale are less pronounced. Under the implicit assumption that assets and number of accounts change by the same proportion, the measured overall economies of scale are not as strong as under the alternative implicit assumption of no relation between asset growth and growth in the number of accounts. As we have seen, however, there may be reasons to question the validity of the specifications using assets per account as a hedonic. Overall, this study highlights the importance of assumptions made about the interactions between assets and the number of accounts and suggests, perhaps, the need for further research on the best approach to the specification of the hedonic variables.

Another shortcoming of the means previously used to study economies of scale is their focus on the behavior of the costs of the individual fund. As we have discussed, when a firm incurs joint and common costs in producing a multiplicity of products, traditional measures of scale economies used in the single output case are no longer legitimate. When such cost complementarities are present, it is impossible to measure the total costs associated with a single output.

Our results also indicate that cost complementarities are present in the mutual fund complex. Significant economies of scope between money market and other mutual funds are observed. Indeed, with our preferred specifications, significant economies of scope are present for virtually all the complexes in our sample. It therefore follows that the costs of one type of fund cannot be measured independently of the costs of the other fund type supplied by the complex.

Overall, our empirical results strongly support the finding of both overall economies of scale and economies of scope. It remains to consider the implications of these findings for the evaluation of fees charged by mutual fund managers. It is, of course, true that investors in all of a complex's funds will and should benefit from the cost savings attributable to the presence of economies of scale and scope. However, there are no precise rules for determining how these cost savings are passed on to shareholders of different funds.

Previous evaluations of mutual fund fees based on the observation that units costs for a particular fund decline as the fund's assets increase ignore these critical issues and are indefensible. First, the cost figures used in such calculations have invariably been based on arbitrary cost allocation techniques such as fully distributed cost. Second, even if the measured costs were to prove representative of the underlying economic costs, the assumption that some known portion (or all) of such decreases in costs should be passed on to investors of a particular fund ignores the fundamental nature of economies of scope. Such economies must be taken into account when assessing the fees charged by mutual fund managers, since the presence of these economies implies that it is impossible to assign unambiguously any particular share of the costs or benefits associated with joint production to an individual fund in a complex. Third, our hedonic analysis established that the total costs incurred by a mutual fund complex depend not only on the level of output but on the specific characteristics of the output. Previous evaluations of mutual fund fees that looked at costs in relation to assets did not take into account the hedonic qualitites of the fund's output. Fourth, caution is needed in interpreting the meaning of overall economies of scale as it applies to a particular fund. The reason is that this new measure assumes all outputs increase by a constant proportion, an assumption which is unlikely to be met by money market and non-money market mutual funds.

If previous approaches were misguided, what then can be said about the proper evaluation of fees for a particular fund? As detailed in the Appendix to Chapter Three, the proper test for excessive fees involves two steps: first, calculating whether or not the overall rate of return of the entire complex is excessive; second, checking whether each and every one of its funds or product lines is making a net contribution toward recovery of fixed and common costs. The second part of this test is equivalent to examining if the revenue of each product line exceeds the incremental cost for that line. It is, of course, from the estimated cost function that one can calculate the incremental costs.

The empirical analysis of the mutual fund cost complex provides a general framework for estimating incremental costs. While the cost functions we have estimated are illustrative of the approach needed, one would not necessarily use our estimates to evaluate any particular complex.[141] In the first instance, for computational convenience we have restricted attention to only two broad product lines. In applying this methodology for purposes of evaluating fees, one would want to make sure that the aggregation over funds within a complex was consistent with the underlying cost structure. Second, as noted earlier, we did not have available a complete enumeration of all complex costs nor did we have data on factor costs. In a fee assessment application, one would need to consider both of these in estimating a proper cost function.

To recapitulate, while the estimates presented in this chapter are not well-suited for the evaluation of fees of any particular complex, the methodology is precisely what is needed. Moreover, our finding of economies of scope strongly suggests that the evaluation of fees without a properly estimated cost function is likely to be seriously misguided.

---

[141] Aside from the reasons given in the text, there is one technical consideration that makes our estimates unsuitable for evaluating incremental costs. In particular, as noted in Chapter Three, such a calculation involves the evaluation of costs when an output level is set equal to zero. The use of the conventional translog cost function is not suited for this calculation. As noted in Appendix A below, there are more complicated estimation methods for dealing with this issue.

APPENDIX A

Complex Selection Criteria

Tables A.1 and A.2 document steps of the complex selection criteria as outlined in Chapter Seven. The difference in the two tables lies in the filter level for the percentage of complex assets that may be in funds with missing data or in funds that have separate administrators and advisers. In Table A.1, a five percent filter level operates; Table A.2 illustrates the effects of a 40 percent filter level.

Referring to Table A.1, there are 1,542 observations in the original sample, where an observation corresponds to a complex for a given year. Of these 1,542 original data points, 224 complexes have funds with statistics that had been reported in an earlier *Directors' Report*; that is, for some funds, the same data were reported for each variable for successive years. The majority of complexes eliminated due to this criterion is attributable to a reporting change in 1987. In that year Lipper apparently moved its publication date from late spring to earlier in the year. As a result, complexes simply reported the previous year's statistics again. For 1987, these complexes were removed from the sample.

Next, complexes having funds missing data or having funds with separate administrators and advisers are eliminated if the percentage of complex assets represented by such funds exceeds the filter level. Thus 805 complexes are eliminated if a five percent filter is used, and 604 complexes are eliminated using a 40 percent filter.

Since the translog specification cannot accommodate zero output levels, complexes offering a single fund type are also eliminated. As shown in Table A.1, an additional 334 complexes are removed at this stage. For the 40 percent filter level, 413 complexes are eliminated at this stage as shown in Table A.2. Finally, 179 complexes remain using the five percent filter, and 301 complexes survive when the 40 percent filter is used.[142]

Of interest is how the surviving complexes compare with the complexes in the original data set. Tables A.3 and A.4 present selected summary statistics of the universe of mutual fund complexes. Sample average complex expenses (taken from Table 7.2) of $9.5 million are comparable to expenses reported in Table A.4.[143] Average complex average net assets of $1,295 million are slightly smaller than those in the universe. Further, complexes surviving the five percent filters have 127,541 accounts on average, which is well within the range of the annual averages presented in Table A.4. In short, although the selection criteria greatly reduced the number of complexes, surviving complexes do not appear to differ from the original complexes.

---

[142] Future research will investigate Box-Cox transformations of the variables. While this approach, which has been used by Caves, Christensen, and Tretheway (1980), involves more complicated nonlinear estimation techniques, it also permits zero output levels. As a result, we would have 513 complexes (five percent filter) or 714 complexes (40 percent filter) available for estimation purposes.

[143] All dollar values are stated in terms of December 1986 dollars.

Table A.1

Selection Criteria, Five Percent Filter

	1982	1983	1984	1985	1986	1987	Total
(1) Number of complexes	181	211	238	268	306	338	1,542
(2) Number of complexes having funds with duplicative data	0	8	8	20	22	166	224
(3) Number of complexes having funds with missing data constituting more than five percent of complex assets[a]	83	110	139	153	187	133	805
(4) Number of complexes offering a single fund type only	61	60	57	60	65	31	334
(5) Number of complexes available for cost function estimation[b]	37	33	34	35	32	8	179

Notes: [a] Missing data means that expenses, number of accounts, assets, or turnover are not available, or that the complex lists administer-only or advise-only funds.
[b] (5) = (1) - (2) - (3) - (4).

Source: Lipper — Directors' Analytical Data.

Table A.2

Selection Criteria, 40 Percent Filter

	1982	1983	1984	1985	1986	1987	Total
(1) Number of complexes	181	211	238	268	306	338	1,542
(2) Number of complexes having funds with duplicative data	0	8	8	20	22	166	224
(3) Number of complexes having funds with missing data constituting more than 40 percent of complex assets[a]	59	78	99	113	140	115	604
(4) Number of complexes offering a single fund type only	74	75	73	74	81	36	413
(5) Number of complexes available for cost function estimation[b]	48	50	58	61	63	21	301

Notes: [a] Missing data means that expenses, number of accounts, assets, or turnover are not available, or that the complex lists administer-only or advise-only funds.
  [b] (5) = (1) - (2) - (3) - (4).

Source: Lipper — Directors' Analytical Data.

Table A.3

Fund Characteristics

Year[b]	Expenses per fund ($ thousands)[a]		Average net assets per fund ($ millions)[a]		Number of accounts per fund	
	N	Average	N	Average	N	Average
1982	584	2,142.0	586	350.9	527	23,161
1983	678	2,555.3	680	420.9	591	26,733
1984	901	2,320.4	903	361.4	683	27,998
1985	1,100	2,087.1	1,100	304.1	811	29,616
1986	1,326	2,184.0	1,330	315.8	930	28,452
1987	1,498	2,418.1	1,502	344.8	981	30,497

Notes: [a] All dollar amounts are in 1986 dollars.
[b] Year is the publication year of the Lipper Directors' Report.

Sources: Economic Report of the President, 1986-1988 editions; Lipper — Directors' Analytical Data.

Table A.4

Complex Characteristics

Year[b]	Expenses per complex ($ thousands)[a]		Average net assets per complex ($ millions)[a]		Number of accounts per complex	
	N	Average	N	Average	N	Average
1982	155	8,070.4	155	1,326.6	152	80,303
1983	175	9,900.1	175	1,635.6	159	99,367
1984	207	10,100.1	208	1,569.1	166	115,197
1985	235	9,769.6	235	1,423.3	181	132,700
1986	263	11,011.2	263	1,596.9	192	137,816
1987	290	12,490.6	290	1,785.9	197	151,865

Notes: [a] All dollar amounts are in terms of 1986 dollars.
        [b] Year is the publication year of the Lipper Directors' Report.

Sources: Economic Report of the President, 1986-1988 editions; Lipper — Directors' Analytical Data.

APPENDIX B

Cost Function Estimation (40 Percent Filter)

Within this appendix, results pertaining to cost estimation using the less restrictive 40 percent filter are presented. Table B.1 presents summary statistics of complexes remaining after the 40 percent filter and other selection criteria are applied. Contrasting Table B.1 and Table A.4, it is readily apparent that the 40 percent filter admits larger complexes on average. For example, average total expenses for this subsample are $17.2 million, or over 65 percent larger than average expenses for the entire sample. Another comparison shows that the average number of accounts is 207,953 for the 40 percent subsample versus 119,541 accounts in the original sample. Other similar comparisons can also be drawn.

Corresponding to Table 7.3 through 7.6 (five percent filter) are Tables B.2 through B.5 (40 percent filter). The signs of estimated coefficients are always the same as their five percent filter counterpart. Perhaps the most important difference is that the turnover rate is always significant in the 40 percent filter models. Given the greater size of the complexes, this is not surprising. For a given turnover rate, these complexes are turning over a larger portfolio on average.

Measures of overall economies of scale and scope evaluated at average output levels are also presented. The reported measures differ only slightly from those presented in Chapter Seven. For example, when the number of accounts is taken to be the output and assets per account are considered a hedonic (Tables 7.7 and B.5), overall economies of scale are 0.871 (five percent filter) and 0.901 (40 percent filter). The measure for economies of scope (Tables 7.9 and B.7) yields 0.040 (five percent filter) and 0.066 (40 percent filter).

In short, estimation results do not appear to be very sensitive to the filter level. However, as pointed out, the five percent filter mimics overall sample averages more closely than the 40 percent filter.

Table B.1

Complexes Offering Both Outputs, 301 Observations, 40 Percent Filter

Variable	Minimum	Maximum	Mean
Total expenses ($ thousands)	450	156,264	17,176
Money market assets ($ thousands)	1,400	22,656,110	1,369,120
Other fund assets ($ thousands)	2,440	12,172,500	1,104,250
Money market assets per account ($)	2,078	384,391	14,996
Other fund assets per account ($)	1,528	48,144	10,090
Number of money market accounts	117	1,125,543	97,883
Number of other fund accounts	80	1,249,166	110,070
Number of money market funds	1.00	13.00	1.65
Number of other funds	1.00	29.00	5.12
Other fund turnover (%)	3.00	418.64	79.92

Note: All dollar amounts are expressed in 1986 constant dollars using the GNP deflator.

Table B.2

Estimation of Cost Function

Output   = Assets
Hedonics = Number of accounts, number of funds, portfolio turnover
Filter   = 40 percent

Variable	Coefficient	t-value
Intercept	16.303	264.74
ln(MM assets)	0.394	17.64
ln(Other assets)	0.278	12.76
ln(Number of MM accounts)	0.101	4.74
ln(Number of other accounts)	0.117	5.84
ln(Number of MM funds)	0.039	1.53
ln(Number of other funds)	0.128	5.05
ln(Turnover)	0.040	3.34
$[\ln(\text{MM assets})]^2$	0.078	30.44
$[\ln(\text{Other assets})]^2$	0.074	23.90
ln(MM assets) x ln(Other assets)	-0.131	-31.77
Number of observations:	301	
Adjusted R-sq.:	0.985	

Table B.3

Estimation of Cost Function

Output   = Assets
Hedonics = Assets per account, number of funds, portfolio turnover
Filter   = 40 percent

Variable	Coefficient	t-value
Intercept	16.296	264.62
ln(MM assets)	0.496	41.68
ln(Other assets)	0.396	27.53
ln(MM assets per account)	-0.101	-4.74
ln(Other assets per account)	-0.117	-5.84
ln(Number of MM funds)	0.039	1.53
ln(Number of other funds)	0.128	5.05
ln(Turnover)	0.040	3.34
$[ln(MM\ assets)]^2$	0.078	30.44
$[ln(Other\ assets)]^2$	0.074	23.90
ln(MM assets) x ln(Other assets)	-0.131	-31.77
Number of observations:	301	
Adjusted R-sq.:	0.985	

```
                              Table B.4

                    Estimation of Cost Function
```

Output = Number of accounts		
Hedonics = Assets, number of funds, portfolio turnover		
Filter = 40 percent		

Variable	Coefficient	t-value
Intercept	16.398	242.09
ln(MM assets)	0.275	11.69
ln(Other assets)	0.264	11.18
ln(Number of MM accounts)	0.203	7.33
ln(Number of other accounts)	0.158	5.91
ln(Number of MM funds)	0.054	1.92
ln(Number of other funds)	0.456	1.63
ln(Turnover)	0.059	4.44
$[\ln(\text{No. of MM accounts})]^2$	0.071	24.40
$[\ln(\text{No. of other accounts})]^2$	0.071	23.08
ln(No. MM accts) x ln(No. other accts)	-0.136	-29.06
Number of observation:	301	
Adjusted R-sq.:	0.982	

Table B.5

Estimation of Cost Function

Output   = Number of accounts
Hedonics = Assets per account, number of funds, portfolio turnover
Filter   = 40 percent

Variable	Coefficient	t-value
Intercept	16.419	242.01
ln(MM assets per account)	0.275	11.69
ln(Other assets per account)	0.264	11.18
ln(Number of MM accounts)	0.479	36.58
ln(Number of other accounts)	0.422	26.79
ln(Number of MM funds)	0.054	1.92
ln(Number of other funds)	0.046	1.63
ln(Turnover)	0.059	4.44
$[\ln(\text{No. of MM accounts})]^2$	0.071	24.40
$[\ln(\text{No. of other accounts})]^2$	0.071	23.08
ln(No. MM accts) x ln(No. other accts)	-0.136	-29.06
Number of observations:	301	
Adjusted R-sq.:	0.982	

Table B.6

Overall Economies of Scale, 40 Percent Filter

| Model specification | At average output levels (t-statistic) | Measure of overall economies of scale | | |
		Median value	Complexes with significant economies of scale	Complexes with significant diseconomies of scale
Output = Assets Hedonic = Number of accounts	0.673 (-12.342)	0.616	301	0
Output = Assets Hedonic = Assets per account	0.892 (-7.134)	0.832	288	0
Output = Number of accounts Hedonic = Assets	0.362 (-20.984)	0.344	301	0
Output = Number of accounts Hedonic = Assets per account	0.901 (-6.108)	0.884	301	0

Notes: All models include number of funds and turnover rate as additional hedonic variables.
[a] t-statistics, computed for the measure of overall economies of scale, test whether constant returns to scale are present.
[b] Significance is determined using a five percent level.

Source: Lipper — Directors' Analytical Data.

Table B.7

Overall Economies of Scope, 40 Percent Filter

Model specification	At average output levels (t-statistic)	Measure of overall economies of scale		
		Median value	Complexes with significant economies of scope	Complexes with significant diseconomies of scope
Output = Assets Hedonic = Number of accounts	-0.021 (-1.887)	-0.079	280	0
Output = Assets Hedonic = Assets per account	0.066 (7.107)	-0.002	127	119
Output = Number of accounts Hedonic = Assets	-0.104 (-12.954)	-0.139	301	0
Output = Number of accounts Hedonic = Assets per account	0.066 (6.613)	0.029	100	165

Notes: All models include number of funds and turnover rate as additional hedonic variables.
[a] t-statistics, computed for the measure of overall economies of scale, test whether constant returns to scale are present.
[b] Significance is determined using a five percent level.

APPENDIX C

Statistical Test of Measures of Overall Economies of Scale and Economies of Scope

In this appendix we describe the derivation of the statistical tests used to measure overall economies of scale and economies of scope. It should be noted that the translog cost function is a second-order Taylor series approximation to an arbitrary cost function.[144] The implicit restrictions of, say, a Cobb-Douglas or Constant Elasticity of Substitution production technology are not embedded in the cost functions used here.

Overall Economies of Scale. The measure of overall economies of scale used here is given by

$$\text{SCALE} = \sum_i \frac{\partial \ln C}{\partial \ln y_i}$$

$$= a_1 + a_2 + d_{12}\,[\ln(y_1) + \ln(y_2)] + 2d_{11}\,\ln(y_1)$$

$$+ 2d_{22}\,\ln(y_2) \tag{C.1}$$

where the terms are as defined in the text. Since output variables are normalized to have mean one, the measure of overall economies of scale at the sample means is simply $a_1 + a_2$. Overall economies of scale are evaluated at sample means as well as for each complex's output levels. To test if overall economies of scale are statistically and significantly different from one, the standard error has to be computed. The estimated coefficients are treated as random variables, while $\ln(y_1)$ and $\ln(y_2)$ are treated as weights. Some additional

---

[144] See M. Denny and M. Fuss, "The Use of Approximation Analysis to Test for Separability and the Existence of Consistent Aggregates," *American Economic Review*, vol. 67, no. 3 (1977), 404-418.

notation should prove helpful. Arrange the coefficients in a vector as

$$\Gamma = [\gamma_i] = [a_1, a_2, d_{11}, d_{22}, d_{12}] \qquad (C.2)$$

Similarly, arrange the weights in a vector as

$$W = [w_j] = [1, 1, 2 \ln (y_1), 2 \ln (y_2), \ln (y_1 y_2)] \qquad (C.3)$$

Then the standard error for the measure of overall economies of scale is given by

$$SE(SCALE) = Var \left[\sum (\partial \ln C / \partial \ln y_j) \right]^{0.50}$$

$$= \left[\sum w_i^2 \, Var(\gamma_i) + 2 \sum_{i < j} \sum w_i w_j \, Cov \, (\gamma_i, \gamma_j) \right]^{0.50} \qquad (C.4)$$

In evaluating economies of scale at the sample means, all expressions $\ln(y_1)$ reduce to zero. In this case,

$$SE(SCALE) = [Var(a_1) + Var(a_2) + 2 \, Cov \, (a_1, a_2)]^{0.50} \qquad (C.5)$$

Economies of Scope. Fuss and Waverman (1981) show that the presence of economies of scope imply

$$\partial^2 C / \partial y_1 \, \partial y_2 \; < \; 0$$

where

$$\frac{\partial^2 C}{\partial y_1 \, \partial y_2} = \frac{C}{y_1 y_2} \left[\frac{\partial \ln C}{\partial \ln y_1} \frac{\partial \ln C}{\partial \ln y_2} + \frac{\partial^2 \ln C}{\partial \ln y_1 \, \partial \ln y_2} \right]$$

$$= \frac{C}{y_1 y_2} (a_1 a_2 + d_{12}) \qquad (C.6)$$

provided that the outputs y_i are normalized to have mean one. Since costs are always positive, the expression $a_1 a_2 + d_{12}$ (SCOPE) is used as a measure of economies of scope.

Expression (C.6) is easily evaluated. However, to determine its significance requires more effort.

Since the measure of economies of scope is a nonlinear function of the estimated coefficients, a Taylor series approximation of the variance is used following Kmenta (1971). Specifically, the standard error of the economies of scope term $a_1 a_2 + d_{12}$ is given by

$$
\begin{aligned}
SE(SCOPE) = [a_2{}^2 \, \text{Var}(a_1) &+ a_1{}^2 \, \text{Var}(a_2) + \text{Var}(d_{12}) \\
&+ 2a_2 \, \text{Cov}(a_1, d_{12}) + 2a_1 \, \text{Cov}(a_2, d_{12}) \\
&+ 2a_1 a_2 \, \text{Cov}(a_1, a_2)]^{0.50}
\end{aligned}
\tag{C.7}
$$

To evaluate economies of scope at the complex level, the a_1 and a_2 terms must be transformed so that the resulting estimates a_1' and a_2' are such that these are the coefficients that would obtain if the output levels had been scaled by that complex's particular output levels. This transformation are given by

$$
a_1' = a_1 + 2 d_{11} \ln (y_1/\bar{y}_1) + d_{12} \ln (y_2/\bar{y}_2)
\tag{C.8}
$$

$$
a_2' = a_2 + 2 d_{22} \ln (y_2/\bar{y}_2) + d_{12} \ln (y_1/\bar{y}_1)
\tag{C.9}
$$

so that the measure of economies of scope is $a_1' \, a_2' + d_{12}$. The standard error of this term is more complicated, but is computed through the same method as given for (C.7).

EIGHT

TOWARD RATIONAL POLICY ON REGULATION OF MUTUAL FUNDS

INTRODUCTION

This book has examined, both conceptually and empirically, the economic merits of the arguments offered in support of the current regulatory and legal structure. It has offered evidence on the behavior of the industry, the behavior of mutual fund consumers, and the consequent ability of advisers to charge excessive fees.

This chapter summarizes our findings on the economic behavior of the industry. It then discusses the implications of these findings for law and regulation. We assess the merits of the current structure, and propose changes that would, in our view, increase the efficiency of mutual funds.

Overall, our policy prescriptions suggest that a considerable dose of mutual fund deregulation will serve the public interest. We do not suggest that the industry should be left entirely to its own devices. The rules against fraud and misrepresentation clearly have an important role to play in providing protection to the public, and they should be enforced vigorously. There are, equally, no grounds on which to exempt any entity in the arena from the workings of the antitrust laws. Moreover, we propose the adoption of somewhat more severe disclosure rules than currently exist. Our proposed disclosure rules would provide investors and other interested parties all the information necessary to ensure that no questionable activities or decisions by advisers or others threaten or actually produce detrimental consequences for the legitimate interests of investors. But beyond vigorous execution of such rules, we see no need for any substantial regulation of the industry. We believe that here, as in other industries such as airlines and banking, unnecessary regulation can cause economic inefficiencies that must ultimately be borne by the public in general and by investors in particular in the form of higher prices.

We do not advocate deregulation at any cost. We believe that in many areas of the economy regulation has an important and continuing role to play. We believe, for example, that in the arena of toxic wastes current regulation is indefensibly weak and that the public interest is severely endangered by the regulatory vacuum. Similarly, we believe that the presence of market power can fully justify continuation of rate regulation, as in the case of rail traffic that serves "captive shippers" in markets where other modes of competition do not effectively constrain the rate decisions of the rail carriers. Thus, the deregulatory recommendations of this chapter should not be attributed to a doctrinaire belief in deregulation as an end in itself. We believe, rather, that they are based on a careful study of the market structure, conduct, and performance of the mutual fund industry.

A REVIEW OF FEE SETTING IN THE MUTUAL FUND INDUSTRY

The Exploitation Hypothesis

Most of the current regulation of mutual funds rests on the assumption that individuals who invest their money in such funds are peculiarly vulnerable to exploitation by the fund's advisers. Critics argue that two features of the structure of mutual funds cause their customers — or shareholders — to be more vulnerable to exploitation than are consumers of other, more prosaic goods and services. These features are (1) captivity of mutual funds by their advisers and (2) the negligible relative size of advisory fees.

The first of these features, it is argued, prevents shareholders from replacing a given mutual fund's adviser. The captivity problem allegedly occurs because funds are the creation of their advisers. The funds are thus bound to the services and strategy selected by that adviser, and hence have no freedom to shop for better terms from rival advisers. Under such a structure, competition among funds for investing customers may be strong and effective, but competition among advisory firms to supply their services to individual funds is alleged to be virtually non-existent. This lack of competition in turn is argued to permit advisers to set fees, disregarding market forces that ordinarily constrain price-setting behavior.

The second structural feature — the small size of advisory fees relative to funds' net yields — is claimed to render shareholders insensitive to the magnitude of fee schedules. Because of this insensitivity, investors allegedly cannot be counted upon to shop among competing funds and thereby prevent supracompetitive fees. A substantial increase in fees has so minuscule an effect on yields that the increase is virtually certain to escape the notice of investors. Consequently, the investors will not undertake the effort required to switch to a competing fund whose advisory fees are lower.

Economic Incentives and Industry Behavior

Our examination of the opportunity for abuse by mutual fund advisers began with a study of the incentives faced by advisers and firms providing services to mutual funds. As we discussed in Chapter Five, the key question is whether the mutual fund adviser has the ability to wield market power. We found that such market power exists if, and only if, there are obstacles that prevent consumers from choosing freely among advisers.

The mutual fund industry can be viewed as a composite of two integrated levels of activity: (1) the market for advisory services, and (2) the market for funds. Advisory services constitute an upstream input into assembly of the final mutual fund product offered to consumers. Viewed in this way, there can be excessive pricing for advisory services only if consumers are prevented from shopping competitively among advisers. The traditional view is that consumers are constrained from such competitive shopping because they can only move among funds. That is, they cannot switch advisers and remain within a given fund.

The traditional view ignores the ability of consumers to shop among advisers by shopping among funds. If there is free entry into the advising business, and if consumers can readily acquire the services of competing advisers by transferring their assets to competing funds, then whether or not a given fund is tied to a particular adviser is irrelevant. The ability to switch among funds provides the same competitive discipline as the ability to switch among advisers within a given fund.

Consequently, our analysis focused on the degree to which consumers have competitive access to different advisory services. We identified two characteristics of industry structure that are essential for low-cost access to different advisory services. The first is whether there is free entry into the advising business. The second is whether the costs to consumers of switching among funds is low. If both of these features are present, then individual advisers must be prevented by competition from charging excessive fees.

The Evidence on Competition for Advisory Services

The evidence we examined leads us to conclude that mutual fund customers can shop freely among competing fund advisers by switching funds at low cost. As Chapter Five showed in detail, our conclusion is supported by a record of strong and consistent entry of both new advisers and new funds into the mutual fund industry. Entry has been particularly dramatic in the past decade. During this period, funds have proliferated. More important, perhaps, many of the new funds have been offered by new advisers. Clearly, there are no effective barriers to entry into either the advisory business or the provision of mutual fund products to consumers.

The rapid expansion of the mutual fund industry, and the resulting proliferation of products and vendors, has driven down the costs that consumers must bear when switching among funds. A variety of costs that previously rendered switching relatively expensive have either diminished or been eliminated entirely. These costs include liquidity, sales loads, and redemption fees. The costs of switching among funds may indeed have been prohibitively high at the time of the Investment Company Act of 1940. But in the modern mutual fund market, competition has driven costs to negligible levels.

Chapter Six provided an analysis of consumers' sensitivity to relative yields, and thus, implicitly, to the relative fees of any individual fund. In that chapter we show that consumer demand for the shares of a given fund is extremely sensitive to relative yield. This sensitivity implies that consumers switch funds readily in response to small changes in relative net yield that stem from either direct performance changes or differences in fees between funds. This evidence documents two important facts. First, switching costs are low. Second, even though fees are small, they are likely to have a significant effect on consumers' fund-purchase decisions.

PROPOSALS FOR A MODIFIED REGULATORY REGIME

The legislation governing the mutual fund industry, notably the Investment Act of 1940 and the related amendments of 1970, are designed to protect investors from abusive conduct by mutual fund advisers. The laws impose a corporate-like structure upon mutual funds, requiring them to be governed by boards of directors who are obligated to represent the public interest. The rules also require ratification of management fees by both the boards of directors and the shareholders of the funds. In addition, the 1970 Amendments to the Investment Company Act impose a direct fiduciary burden on mutual fund advisers. One can describe the broad regulatory structure imposed on the mutual fund industry as one in which every fund is endowed with its own mini-regulatory agency. The "regulators" associated with the fund — its outside directors — have the power to accept or reject any proposed fees regardless of current market conditions.

A great deal of weight has been attached to the governing authority of mutual fund directors. As described in Chapter Three, the outcomes of many of the lawsuits alleging excess fees have depended critically on (1) whether the directors of the funds had been provided with all pertinent information and (2) whether that information had been deliberated over adequately by the directors before they acquiesced to the fees. The lawsuits complaining about mutual fund advisory fees have further intensified the regulatory-agency atmosphere of the fee-determination process.   They have brought into the field all the ancient regulatory baggage now discredited in such industries as rail and telecommunications. The lawsuits have pressured directors into employing arbitrary but traditional regulatory devices such as fully distributed cost in their oversight of the fee-setting structure.

As an alternative to these arbitrary regulatory devices, we offer the following proposals:

1. Elimination of the regulations contained in the 1940 Investment Company Act governing the level of advisory fees and earnings
2. Elimination of the requirement that the funds be governed by a corporate-like structure
3. Continuation and perhaps even strengthening of the current disclosure requirements
4. A re-examination and perhaps elimination of current arrangements that serve to impede the mobility of investors among funds

We now discuss each of these proposals in turn.

Eliminating the Special Pricing and Earnings Evaluation Criteria in the 1940 Investment Company Act

In markets as competitive as those for mutual fund adviser services, any legal rules that invite the intervention of the courts beyond the extent to which they are necessary to deter fraud are sure to distort the pricing process. Such pricing rules often induce the imposition of prices other than those that the forces of competition would have yielded. Consequently, the resulting industry prices will not be those that best serve the public interest.

In addition, such legal rules impose the substantial costs of unnecessary litigation. Where the pertinent laws and legal precedents impose special rules and procedures upon the pricing process, administrative costs are sure to be magnified and inefficiencies exacerbated.

Accordingly, we urge Congress to eliminate all special regulatory-like provisions affecting the pricing of advisory services. Coupled with this elimination should be a strong reaffirmation of (1) the applicability of the antitrust laws and (2) the laws against fraud.

Eliminating the Imposition of a Corporate-like Structure upon Mutual Funds

As we have already discussed, the competitiveness of the mutual fund industry eliminates the need for an elaborate and costly governance structure within individual mutual funds. The structure imposed by the 1940 Act, requiring each adviser to secure approval of its fee structures from a board including a prespecified proportion of outside representatives, is unnecessary if market discipline prevents advisers from charging excess fees. Since this is in fact so, the review mechanisms imposed by the 1940 Act constitute a costly burden that decreases both the efficiency of mutual fund markets and consumer welfare.

For this reason, we would strongly urge elimination of the governance requirements. That would leave funds free to choose the most effective and efficient organizational structure with which to compete in the marketplace. That can only benefit consumers of mutual fund services.

Disclosure Requirements

Our analysis does not provide any evidence that calls for a weakening of current disclosure requirements for mutual funds and their advisers. Indeed, it may be desirable to strengthen the current requirements to increase the power of the market to constrain fees appropriately. In particular, we recommend consideration of two amendments of the current procedures.

1. Rules should be designed that create uniform performance reporting. Such rules should facilitate interfund comparisons by consumers.

2. Rules should be adopted that require periodic fund reporting to shareholders of fund performance, portfolio composition, advisory fees, and total expenses. The reporting of portfolio composition will facilitate evaluation of a fund's riskiness by prospective and actual investors. The reporting of expenses will help consumers make informed choices about service-yield tradeoffs. Since funds differ in the range and quality of the services they offer, differences in yields may be attributable either to differences in the quality of manager performance or to variations in services provided. Expense information, albeit a highly imperfect indicator, may help investors to arrive at a rational judgment on the matter.

Facilitating Investor Ability to Move from One Fund to Another

Since the effectiveness of the competitive mechanism in the market for the services of mutual funds rests on the ability of investors to punish poor fund performance by voting with their dollars, any impediments to investor mobility among funds must be held to a minimum. Chapter Five showed, for example, that front-end and back-end loading by funds constitutes a market impediment, because such loading increases the cost of switching from one fund to another. The same is true of the requirement that redemptions must exceed some fixed minimum amount of money.

We are not prepared to go so far as to suggest prohibition of all such arrangements. However, at the very least, such arrangements should be subject to a clear disclosure requirement, clearly comprehensible to a lay person, that indicates the nature of the impediment to mobility that these arrangements entail. Small first-time investors in such a fund should be given a brief period of grace after receipt of this statement to withdraw their investments without financial penalty. This should help to ensure maximization of investor mobility.

Finally, we would encourage the search for other changes that promise to reduce the volume of unnecessary and costly litigation. It is at least arguable that some lawyers and investors in funds have interpreted the current arrangements to constitute a promising opportunity to milk the funds or the advisory firms through lawsuits. Of course, since the other customers predictably end up paying the legal costs, such litigation activity forces the transfer of wealth from one group to another. The litigation opportunity encourages what economists refer to as rent-seeking activity, which many believe to constitute a prime source of inefficiency in our economy.

CONCLUSIONS

Investors have much at stake in the proposals we have just discussed. The simplification of business operations permitted by deregulation will increase investor returns. This is the lesson of experience in other arenas where deregulation has occurred. Curiously, the regulated firms themselves stand to gain little from deregulation, since the competitiveness of the market for funds will ensure that any gains in profits are soon passed on to the investing public. Our proposals, then, cannot be interpreted as an attempt to promote some special business interests. Consumers of financial services are the prospective gainers.

We conclude with two final comments. First, observers of the mutual fund industry should exercise care in interpreting fee structures that differ from adviser to adviser. The presence of a variety of fee structures in different mutual funds does not imply that any of them need constitute exploitation. Rather, such disparities may correspond to differences in performance and service characteristics. Funds with superior performance should be permitted by the market to offer high payments to their managers, which must be interpreted as the market's normal reward for superior performance. After all, if such rewards are declared illegitimate, and are ruled out by regulation, what incentive is left for management to devote extraordinary effort to superior performance? Indeed, failure to permit such incentives in other regulated arenas explains much of their poor productivity performance.

Finally, if advisory fees cause only minimal and virtually unobservable differences to fund yields, then any cost-benefit test should raise strong doubts about the justifiability of imposing a costly and stultifying regime of regulation merely to prevent what, by hypothesis, is so insignificant a transgression. If the primary result of such regulation is a diversion of managerial energy and an increase in the costs of operation, then the regulations cannot be justified even if the problem exists. The interests of shareholders are better served by allowing the market to function freely and to limit the opportunity for abuse. When compared to a regulatory regime, the market-based solution ensures at least that the cure will not be more costly than the disease.

BIBLIOGRAPHY

Acampora v. Birkland. 220 Federal Supplement 527 (D. Colo. 1963).

Advertising News Service, Inc. *Bank Rate Monitor.*

Ang, James S., and Jess H. Chua. "Mutual Funds: Different Strokes for Different Folks?" *Journal of Portfolio Management*, vol. 8, no. 2 (Winter, 1982), 43-47.

Bailey, Elizabeth E., and William J. Baumol. "Deregulation and the Theory of Contestable Markets," *Yale Journal on Regulation*, vol 1, no. 2 (1984), 111-137.

Baumol, W.J. "On the Proper Tests for Natural Monopoly in a Multiproduct Industry," *American Economic Review*, vol. 67 (December, 1977), 809-822.

Baumol, W.J., and Y.M. Braunstein. "Empirical Study of Scale Economies and Production Complementarity: The Case of Journal Publication," *Journal of Political Economy*, vol. 85 (October, 1977), 1037-1048.

Baumol, W.J., J. Panzar, and R. Willig. *Contestable Markets and the Theory of Market Structure* (New York: Harcourt, Brace & Jovanovich, 1982), and revised edition, (San Diego: Harcourt, Brace & Jovanovich, 1988).

Benedict, James N., and Mark Holland. "Standards of Fiduciary Duty Under Section 36(b) of the Investment Company Act," *New Dimensions in Securities Litigation: Planning and Strategies*, ALI-ABA Course of Study (1987).

Benston, G.J. "Economies of Scale in Financial Institutions," *Journal of Money, Credit and Banking*, vol. 4 (May, 1972), 319-354.

Benston, G.J., G. Hanweck, and D. Humphrey. "Scale Economies in Banking: A Restructuring and Reassessment," *Journal of Money, Credit and Banking*, vol. 14 (November, 1982), 435-456.

Bull and Bear Capital Growth Fund, Inc. Prospectus (May 1, 1988).

Butler's Money Fund Report, (December, 1975-1976), [see *Donoghue's Money Fund Reports*].

Caves, D.W., L.R. Christensen, and M.W. Tretheway. "Flexible Cost Functions for Multiproduct Firms," *Review of Economics and Statistics*, vol. 62 (August, 1980), 477-481.

Christensen, L.R., D.W. Jorgenson, and L.J. Lau. "Transcendental Logarithmic Production Functions," *Review of Economics and Statistics*, vol. 55 (January, 1973), 28-45.

Clark, J.A. "Economies of Scale and Scope at Depository Financial Institutions," *Economic Review*, Federal Reserve Bank of Kansas City, vol. 73, no. 8, (September/October, 1988), 16-33.

"Conference Report No. 91-1631, November 25, 1970," *Congressional Record*, vol. 116 (1970), 4943-4948.

"Conflict of Interest in the Allocation of Mutual Fund Brokerage Business," *Yale Law Journal*, vol. 80 (1970-1971), 372-394.

Cook, Timothy Q., and Jeremy G. Duffield. "Average Costs of Money Market Mutual Funds," *Economic Review of the Federal Reserve Bank of Richmond* (July/August, 1979), 32-39.

Cook, Timothy Q., and Jeremy G. Duffield. "Money Market Mutual Funds: A Reaction to Regulations or a Lasting Financial Innovation?" *Economic Review of the Federal Reserve Bank of Richmond* (July/August, 1979), 15-31.

Court, A.T. *The Dynamics of Automobile Demand* (New York: General Motors Corporation, 1939).

Denny, M., and M. Fuss. "The Use of Approximation Analysis to Test for Separability and the Existence of Consistent Aggregates," *American Economic Review*, vol. 67, no. 3 (1977), 404-418.

Donoghue Organization, Inc., *Donoghue's Mutual Fund Almanac*, 1981-1988 editions.

Donoghue Organization, Inc., *Donoghue's Money Fund Reports*, (December, 1977-1988 editions), [formerly *Butler's Money Fund Reports*].

Dotsey, Michael, Steven Englander, and John C. Partain. "Money Market Mutual Funds and Monetary Control," *Quarterly Review of the Federal Reserve Bank of New York* (Winter, 1981-1982), 9-17.

Dunham, Constance. "The Growth of Money Market Funds," *New England Economic Review*, vol. 12, no. 5 (September/October, 1980), 20-34.

Economic Report of the President (Washington, D.C.:   U.S. Government   Printing   Office,   1987-1989)   1986-1988 editions.

Frank J. Evangelist, Jr. v. Fidelity Management and Research Company and Fidelity Cash Reserves, Plaintiff's Trial Memorandum,   U.S.   District   Court,   District   of Massachusetts. Civil Action Suit Nos. 81-536-Z and 82-912-Z.

Frank J. Evangelist, Jr. v. Fidelity Management and Research Company and Fidelity Cash Reserves, Defendant's Trial Memorandum,   U.S.   District   Court,   District   of Massachusetts. Civil Action Suit Nos. 81-536-Z and 82-912-Z.

Fama, Eugene. *Foundations of Finance* (New York: Basic Books, 1976).

Fama, Eugene, and Merton Miller. *The Theory of Finance* (New York: Holt, Rinehart, and Winston, 1972).

Federal Reserve Bank Bulletin.

Federal Reserve Statistical Release, H-6, December 17, 1987.

Fidelity Management and Research, "Status of Management Fee Litigation," internal company report, (1986).

Flannery, M. "Correspondent Services and Cost Economies in Commercial   Banking,"   unpublished   manuscript, University of Pennsylvania (1981).

Fogel v. Chestnutt, 533 F.2d 731 (2d Cir. 1975), cert. denied, 429 U.S. 824 (1976).

Fogel v. Chestnutt, 628 F. 2d 100 (2d Cir. 1981) cert. denied, 459 U.S. 828 (1982).

Frankel, Tamar. "Money Market Funds," *The Review of Securities Regulation*, vol. 14, no. 10 (May 20, 1981), 913-924.

Frankel, Tamar. *The Regulation of Money Managers*, (Boston: Little Brown, 1980), vol. 2, ch. 11, 241-304.

Friedlaender, A.F., C. Winston, and K. Wang. "Costs, Technology, and Productivity in the U.S. Automobile Industry," *Bell Journal of Economics*, vol. 14 (Spring, 1983), 1-20.

Fuss, M., and L. Waverman. "Regulation and the Multiproduct Firm: The Case of Telecommunications in Canada," G. Fromm, ed., *Studies in Public Regulation* (Cambridge: MIT Press, 1981).

Galfand v. Chestnutt Corp. 545 F.2d 807 (2d Cir. 1976), cert. denied, 435 U.S. 943 (1978).

Gartenberg v. Merrill Lynch Asset Management, Inc., et al., and *Andre v. Merrill Lynch Ready Assets Trust, et al.* 528 Federal Supplement 1038 (1981). U.S. District Court, S.D.N.Y. Nos. 79 Civ. 3123(MP), 79 Civ. 5726(MP). December 28, 1981.

Gartenberg v. Merrill Lynch Asset Management, Inc., et al., and *Andre v. Merrill Lynch Ready Assets Trust, et al.* 573 Federal Supplement 1293 (1983). U.S. District Court, S.D. N.Y. Nos. 82 Civ. 8074(MP), 81 Civ. 7021(MP). September 1, 1983.

Gartenberg v. Merrill Lynch Asset Management, Inc., et al., and *Andre v. Merrill Lynch Ready Assets Trust, et al.* 694 Federal Reporter, 2nd Series 923 (1982). U.S. Court of Appeals, Second Circuit. Nos. 11, 14, Dockets 82-7142, 82-7074. Argued September 15, 1982. Decided December 3, 1982.

Gartenberg v. Merrill Lynch Asset Management, Inc., et al. 740
    Federal Reporter, 2nd Series 190 (1984). U.S. Court of
    Appeals, Second Circuit. No. 1155, Docket 83-7824.
    Argued April 30, 1984. Decided July 25, 1984.

Gilligan, Thomas, Michael Smirlock, and William Marshall.
    "Scale and Scope Economies in the Multiproduct
    Banking Firm," *Journal of Monetary Economics*, vol. 13,
    no. 3 (1984), 393-405.

Gillis, John G. "What is a Fair Fee?" *Financial Analysts Journal*
    (March/April, 1982), 17-20.

Glazer, Donald W. "A Study of Mutual Fund Complexes,"
    University of Pennsylvania Law Review, vol. 119
    (Decemeber, 1970), 205-281.

Goldfeld, S.M. "Savings and Loan Associations and the Market
    for Savings," *A Study of the Savings and Loan Industry*,
    vol. 2, I. Friend, ed., Federal Home Loan Bank Board
    (1969), 569-658.

Herman, Edward S. "Lobell on the Wharton School Study of
    Mutual Funds: A Rebuttal," *Virginia Law Review*, vol.
    49, no. 1 (1963), 938-962.

The Institute for Econometric Research. "Money Fund Safety
    Ratings," issue no. 53 (December, 1985).

Investment Company Act of 1940.

"Investment Company Act Release No. 12888, December 10,
    1982," *Federal Securities Law Reports*, vol. 999
    (December 21, 1982), 85613-85640.

Investment Company Institute. *Mutual Fund Fact Book*, 1984-
    1988 editions (Washington, D.C.: 1985-1989).

Investment Company Institute. *Trends in Mutual Fund Activity* (Washington D.C.: March, 1985).

Jorgenson, D.W. "Econometric Methods for Modeling Producer Behavior," *Handbook of Econometrics*, vol. 3, Z. Griliches and M. Intriligator, eds. (Amsterdam: North-Holland, 1986).

Kamen v. Kemper Financial Services, Inc., et al. 659 Federal Supplement 1153 (N.D.Ill. 1987). U.S. District Court, N.D. Illinois, E.D. No. 85 C 4587. February 2, 1982.

Kim, Tye. "An Assessment of the Performance of Mutual Fund Management: 1969-1975," *Journal of Financial and Quantitative Analysis*, vol. 13, no. 3 (1978), 385-406.

Klein, Benjamin. "Transaction Cost Determinants of 'Unfair' Contractual Arrangements," *American Economic Review*, vol. 70 (May, 1980), 356-362.

Klein, Benjamin, R.A. Crawford, and A.A. Alchian. "Vertical Integration, Appropriable Rents, and the Competitive Contracting Process," *Journal of Law and Economics*, vol. 21 (October, 1978), 297-326.

Jeffrey Krinsk v. Fund Asset Management, Inc., et al. U.S. District Court, S.D.N.Y. 85 Civ. 8428 (JMW). June 27, 1988.

Lakonishok, Josef. "Performance of Mutual Funds Versus Their Expenses," *Journal of Bank Research*, vol. 11 (Summer, 1981), 110-113.

Landes, William M., and Richard A. Posner. "Market Power in Antitrust Cases," *Harvard Law Review*, vol. 94, no. 5 (1981), 937-996.

Lewellen, Wilbur G., Ronald C. Lease, and Gary G. Schlarbaum. "Some Evidence on the Patterns and Causes of Mutual Fund Ownership," *Journal of Economics and Business*, vol. 30, no. 1 (1977), 57-67.

Lipper Analytical Securities Corporation. *Lipper — Directors' Analytical Data* (Spring, 1982-1987).

Lobell, Nathan D. "A Critique of the Wharton School Report on Mutual Funds," *Virginia Law Review*, vol. 49 (January, 1963), 1-57.

Lyon, Andrew B. "Money Market Funds and Shareholder Dilution," *The Journal of Finance*, vol. 39, no. 4 (September, 1984), 1011-1020.

MacAvoy, Paul W., and Kenneth Robinson. "Winning by Losing: The AT&T Settlement and Its Impact on Telecommunications," *Yale Journal on Regulation*, vol. 1, no. 1 (1983), 1-42.

Magill, Michael J. P. "The Preferability of Investment Through a Mutual Fund," *Journal of Economic Theory*, vol. 13 (October, 1976), 264-271.

Maisel, Sherman, and Kenneth Rosen. "The Macroeconomics of Money Market Mutual Funds," Center for Real Estate and Urban Economics, University of California at Berkeley, Working Paper 82-56 (December, 1982).

Meiselman v. Eberstadt, 39 Del. Ch. 563, 170 A.2d 720 (1961).

Meyer v. Oppenheimer Management Corporation, et al. 764 Federal Reporter, 2nd Series 76 (1985). U.S. Court of Appeals, Second Circuit. No. 920, Docket 84-7977. Argued April 1, 1985. Decided May 30, 1985.

Murray, John D., and Robert W. White. "Economies of Scale and Economies of Scope in Multiproduct Financial Institutions: A Study of British Columbia Credit Unions," *Journal of Finance*, vol. 38 (June, 1983), 887-902.

"The Mutual Fund Industry: A Legal Survey," *Notre Dame Lawyer*, vol. 44 (1968-1969) 732-794.

North, Walter P. "A Brief History of Federal Investment Company Legislation," *Notre Dame Lawyer*, vol. 44 (1968-1969), 677-698.

Nutt, William J. "A Study of Mutual Fund Independent Directors," *University of Pennsylvania Law Review*, vol. 120, no. 2 (1971), 179-270.

Ordover, Janusz A., Alan O. Sykes, and R.D. Willig. "Herfindahl Concentration, Rivalry, and Mergers," *Harvard Law Review*, vol. 95, no. 8 (1982), 1857-1874.

Panzar, John C., and Robert D. Willig. "Economies of Scope," *AEA Papers and Proceedings* (May, 1981), 268-272.

Papilsky v. Berndt, [1976-1977 Transfer Binder] Fed. Sec. L. Report (CCH) Para. 95, 627 (S.D.N.Y. June 24, 1976).

Pepper v. Litton, 308 U.S. 295, 306-07, 60 S.Ct. 238, 245-46, 84 L. Ed. 281 (1939).

Phillips, Richard M. "Deregulation Under the Investment Companies Act — A Reevaluation of the Corporate Paraphernalia of Shareholder Voting and Boards of Directors," *The Business Lawyer*, vol. 37 (April, 1982), 903-913.

"Regulating Risk Taking By Mutual Funds," *Yale Law Journal*, vol. 82 (1972-1973), 1305-1324.

Rogers, William P., and James N. Benedict. "Money Market
    Mutual Fund Management Fees: How Much is Too
    Much?" *New York University Law Review*, vol. 57, no. 6
    (1982), 1059-1125.

Rosen, Kenneth T., and Larry Katz. "Money Market Mutual
    Funds: An Experiment in Ad Hoc Deregulation: A
    Note," *The Journal of Finance*, vol. 38, no. 5 (June,
    1983), 1101-1017.

Rottenberg, Alan W. "Developing Limits on Compensation of
    Mutual Fund Advisers," *Harvard Journal on Legislation*,
    vol. 7, no. 2 (1970), 309-355.

Saxe v. Brady, 40 Del. Ch. 474, 184 A.2d 602 (1962).

Securities Act of 1933.

Securities and Exchange Commission. *Payment of Asset-Based
    Sales Loads by Registered Open-End Management
    Investment Companies.* 17 CRF Part 239, 270, 274,
    Release No. IC-16431; File No. S7-10-88.

Securities and Exchange Commission. *Outline of New
    Investment Company Advertising Rules* (Washington D.C.:
    U.S. Government Printing Office, January 28, 1988).

Securities and Exchange Commission. "Payment of Asset-Based
    Sales Loads by Registered Open-End Management
    Investment Companies," 17 CFR, Part 239, 270, 274,
    release no. IC-16431, file no. 57-10-88 (Washington D.C.:
    U.S. Government Printing Office, June 13, 1988), 1-5.

Securities and Exchange Commission. "Public Policy
    Implications of Investment Company Growth," *Report of
    the Committee on Interstate and Foreign Commerce*
    (Washington D.C.: U.S. Government Printing Office,
    December 2, 1966).

Securities and Exchange Commission. *Report of the Staff of the Division of Investment Management of the Securities and Exchange Commission on the Regulation of Money Market Funds* (Washington D.C.: U.S. Government Printing Office, January 24, 1980).

Securities Exchange Act of 1934.

Senate Report No. 91-184, "Investment Company Amendments Act of 1970," 91st Congress, 2nd Session (1970), 4897-4903.

Schuyt v. Rowe Price Prime Reserve Fund, et al. 622 Federal Supplement 169 (D.C.N.Y. 1985). U.S. District Court, S.D. N.Y. No. 80 Civ. 506 (RJW). November 5, 1985.

Schuyt v. Rowe Price Prime Reserve Fund, et al. 663 Federal Supplement 962 (S.D.N.Y. 1987). U.S. District Court, S.D. New York. No. 80 Civ. 506 (RJW). July 1, 1987.

Siconolfi, Michael. "SEC is Studying Cost Differences of Mutual Funds," *The Wall Street Journal* (June 22, 1988), 37.

Shapiro, Carl. "Consumer Information, Product Quality, and Seller Reputation," *The Bell Jounral of Economics*, vol. 13, no. 1 (Spring, 1982) 20-35.

Shawky, Hany, Ronald Forbes, and Alan Frankle. "Liquidity Services and Capital Market Equilibrium: The Case for Money Market Mutual Funds," *The Journal of Financial Research*, vol. 6, no. 2 (Summer, 1983) 141-152.

Spady, R.H., and A.F. Friedlaender. "Hedonic Cost Functions for the Regulated Trucking Industry," *Bell Journal of Economics*, vol. 9 (Spring, 1978), 159-179.

Tannebaum v. Zeller, 552 F.2d 402 (2d Cir.), cert. denied, 434 U.S. 934 (1977).

U.S. Department of Justice, *Merger Guidelines*, Section 3.1 (June 14, 1984).

Varian, H.R. *Microeconomic Analysis* (New York: W.W. Norton & Company, 1978).

von Weizsacker, C.C. "A Welfare Analysis of Barriers to Entry," *The Bell Journal of Economics*, vol. 11, no. 2 (Autumn, 1980), 399-420.

Wharton School of Finance and Commerce. "A Study of Mutual Funds," *House Report* No. 2274, 87th Congress, 2nd Session (Washington D.C.: U.S. Government Printing Office, 1962).

Wiesenberger Financial Services. *Investment Companies* (New York: 1976).

Williamson, Oliver E. *The Economic Institutions of Capitalism* (New York: The Free Press, Macmillan, Inc., 1985).

Willig, R.D. "Multiproduct Technology and Market Structure," *American Economic Review*, vol. 69 (May, 1979), 346-351.

Wolfson v. Stein, Roe and Farnham [1976-1977] Fed. Sec. L. Rep. (CCH) Para. 95,634 (S.D.N.Y. June 22, 1976), aff'd without opinion sub nom., no. 76-7382 (2d Cir. 1977).

INDEX